RY

by Dick McClary

Illustrations by Andrew Simpson

First Published 2009
The Royal Yachting Association
RYA House, Ensign Way, Hamble
Southampton SO31 4YA
Tel: 0845 345 0400
Fax: 0845 345 0329
E-mail: publications@rya.org.uk
Web: www.rya.org.uk
ISBN: 978-1906-435-028
RYA Order Code: G72

Totally Chlorine Free *Sustainable Forests*

A CIP record of this book is available from the British Library.

Edited by: Andrew Simpson

Cover Design: Pete Galvin

Typesetting and Design: Kevin Slater

Proofreading and indexing: Alan Thatcher

Printed in China through World Print

FOREWORD

When I first became involved in the production of this book, I had no inkling of how deeply it would influence me. To that point I had been a lethargic fisherman, devoid of real interest and certainly of expertise. When bored I would dig out a handline, bought from a tourist shop by the quay. It comprised a plastic frame, thirty metres or so of tatty polypropylene twine, a small weight and a spinner more rust than metal. My seaweed catcher, I called it, for it caught little else. Granted, I had the occasional success. The odd misguided mackerel made it to the pan. But there was never anything to brag about. Little did I know help was just round the corner.

Now, I have known Dick McClary for over 20 years. We're good friends. I even designed his boat and we're still good friends. It was he who led me astray by luring me into a tackle shop. And, for that, he has a lot to answer for.

'What you need is this,' he said, taking a rod from a rack. 'And this ... and ... yup, this.' A reel and other bits of kit were accumulating on the counter. My wallet had developed a dull ache. A further fifteen minutes saw us marching out of the door, myself now booted and spurred like a proper angler.

I would like to be able to report that this was the dawn of a glorious piscatorial career but that was not the case. I tried – oh, how I tried. But the quarry below my keel remained as elusive as ever. For a couple of seasons I soldiered on until, teetering on the brink of total dejection, I contacted Dick.

'What bait are you using?' he asked.

'Oh, bacon rind and things...'

'Bacon rind!' He was clearly appalled. 'And I trust some scrambled eggs and a fried tomato! D'you really think fish wake up yearning for a full English breakfast?'

So, that's where I was going wrong. Suddenly I realised that having the right equipment is not enough. It's like giving a bloke a Stradivarius and expecting him to become a violinist overnight. It's the knowledge that's missing, dummy – the knowledge!

Which brings me back to this book. A couple of years of regular association has drawn me into a world once closed to me. Dick's vast experience and his clarity of expression has turned me from crass beginner to respectable practitioner. And, since it's all so simple once explained, it's left me wondering why on earth it took me so long to get to grips with it.

But, of course, I hadn't read the book then, had I?

Andrew Simpson

INTRODUCTION

The information in this book is drawn from experience gained fishing in northern European coastal waters, the Mediterranean, an Atlantic crossing and the Caribbean. Although some of the examples might seem exotic, one of the lessons that emerges is that the basic principles have almost universal application. For example, the same tackle might catch a mackerel in the UK, a gilthead bream off Greece or a mahi-mahi in the West Indies. Jigging in the English Channel might bring you a nice cod or flounder while it could be a red snapper that goes into the pan off Antigua.

The fact is that sea angling is a very portable activity. The skills that bring success in one place will attract similar rewards even at the other side of the world. It's not where you do it but how you do it that's the real secret.

CONTENTS

CHAPTER 1

THERE FOR THE EATING

Ask any sailor about fishing and he'll have something to say about it. Some will tell you that it's a waste of time and others of the wonderful fish they regularly pluck from the sea. I'm guessing that if you are one of the former you would prefer to join the 'regular catchers' club and I hope that the following chapters will help you gain full membership.

Without a little skill and knowledge, the odds of success are low, except for those odd occasions when Lady Luck swings by. But you can easily acquire those skills and will be richly rewarded as a result. For the long-distance sailor the fresh protein will make a valuable contribution to the dietary needs of his crew, and along the coast what better than a succulent bass to serve up to a hungry crew after a day at sea? In addition, we can all benefit from the Omega fatty acids provided by oily fish like mackerel and tuna, which are said to greatly reduce the chance of heart disease. So why be content with the cans of sardines and tuna that shoal in the darker reaches of your galley when the real thing is available just over the transom?

But trailing a rusty lure around the ocean in the belief that it will be snapped up gleefully is likely to lead to disappointment. If your lure or bait doesn't look like, taste like or behave like familiar food, then your fish is likely to draw the conclusion that it probably isn't and will swim on to dine elsewhere.

Presentation is everything. Even the most delicious morsel impaled on a brutally large hook and suspended on a thick line will create suspicion and an immediate loss of appetite in the fish. Conversely, the same bait on an undersized hook and too light a line is likely to be grabbed gratefully – but by what you'll never know.

An instinctive distrust of anything appearing unnatural is a fish's key defence against an early date with the food chain. They are specialists, not prone to experimentation or conscious risk taking. Self-preservation is their thing and, to catch them, stealth and seduction must be yours. So if you have fished and failed you are very likely going about it the wrong way. The odds are that you've been sussed – it's time to change your approach.

Knowledge of your quarry's likes and dislikes, together with some tweaks to your tackle and techniques will go a long way to getting results. As your skills improve, the rapturous delight previously brought about by a mackerel flapping around on the cockpit sole will begin to pall, and the delicious sea-bass will become your target.

Forays further offshore will turn your thoughts to bonito, skipjack and other members of the tuna family.

And if your cruising ambitions take you south to the Mediterranean or the tropical seas beyond, feeding birds or shoals of panicked flying fish will have you reaching for your heaviest gear in anticipation of the glorious dorado, wahoo or kingfish there beneath them for the taking.

At anchor, other opportunities arise. Maybe a succulent flatfish or two? Or perhaps a hefty seabream or snapper?

But what will it cost to regularly enjoy the delicious flavours of really freshly caught fish? Surprisingly little – about the price you would pay for a few dull-eyed supermarket trout will get you started.

So, fair winds, following seas .... and tight lines.

CHAPTER 2

Fishing underway

Many species of fish spend their lives poking around on the seabed, where marine worms, crustaceans and molluscs make up a large part of their diet. In the absence of a trawl net – an unlikely item on any cruising yacht's inventory – we can forget about these 'demersal' fish, as they are known, until we drop anchor. But other species that operate closer to the surface, feeding on squid, sand eels and smaller fish are a different matter. These include the 'pelagic' fishes, the hunters that patrol the seas in search of their prey, which with a little know-how and some surprisingly simple gear are there for the taking.

TROLLING

Trailing an artificial lure behind the boat, a technique known as 'trolling', can catch these fish. The movement of the lure through the water gives it a life-like action, deceiving fish into thinking it's the real thing. The inconvenience of finding natural bait doesn't arise, making trolling the ideal technique for the cruising yachtsman.

Most long distance skippers keep a trolling line handy, knowing that on passage there is no better source of fresh protein than fish. Off the coasts of Britain and France mackerel, garfish and bass will be the most frequent species to fall to your trolling line. These species arrive in the relatively shallow waters of the European continental shelf during early spring, and depart in the autumn to winter in deep offshore waters of the Western Approaches and beyond. They make good eating – even the garfish, despite its rather uninviting green bones. But the prize catch, from a culinary point of view, is the bass. Distributed throughout our home waters, they are found in greatest numbers off the south and west coasts from southern Scotland around to Norfolk. Ireland also carries a healthy stock but, again, they are most prevalent off the south and west coasts. Bass are also resident along the coasts of France, Spain, Portugal, North Africa and throughout the Mediterranean.

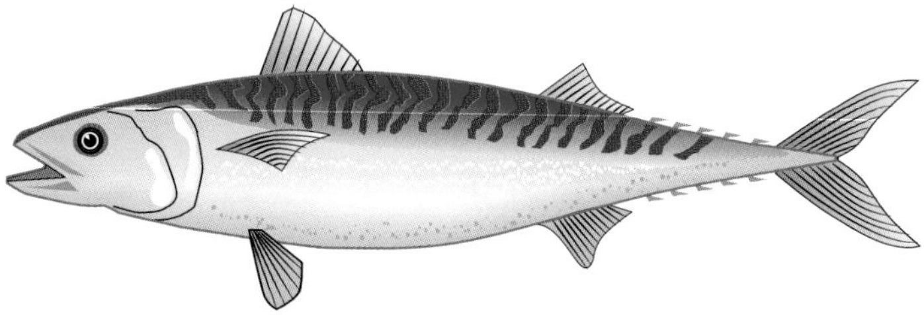

'Mackerel are plentiful and very easy to catch. The quicker they make it to the frying pan or barbecue, the more delicious they will be.

External anatomy of a fish (bass)

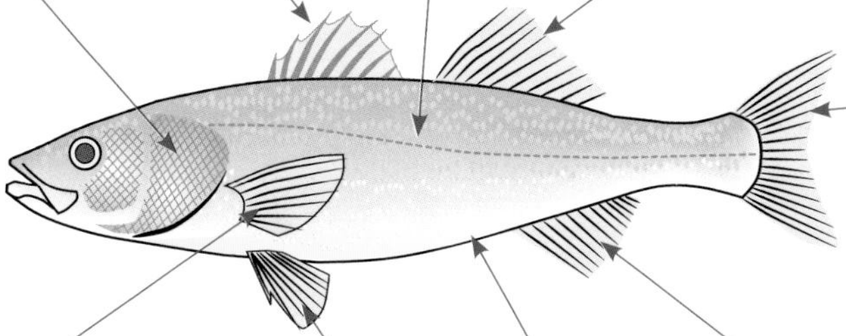

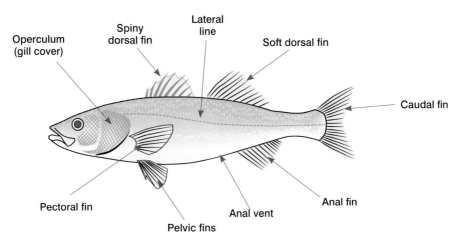

In deeper waters, and particularly where the ocean floor drops off the continental shelf, catching a tuna becomes a realistic prospect. One such 'drop-off' is around latitude 47°N in the Bay of Biscay where the sea bed drops from some 200m to over 1000m in just a few miles. Not the ideal place to be in a south-westerly blow, but a likely spot for a tuna strike on your trolling line.

Off the Atlantic coasts of Spain and Portugal, oceanic depths are found within a few miles of the coastline. Here bonito and skipjack tuna – either of which will fall to an appropriately sized lure – prey voraciously upon huge shoals of sardines. Larger tuna, a bluefin maybe, will eye up your lure as you turn east at Cape St Vincent and through the Straits of Gibraltar into the warm waters of the Mediterranean Sea, there perhaps to catch the delicious albacore.

Those venturing further south to Madeira and onwards to the Canaries will be sailing in waters that big-game anglers pay hefty sums for the privilege of trolling for blue marlin and other large billfish. But you'll probably want to avoid these monsters and direct your attention to the dorado, tuna, albacore, amberjack and wahoo that abound far offshore – perhaps supplementing your diet during a trade wind crossing of the Atlantic Ocean.

Then, trolling a line in the warm waters of the Caribbean, particularly on the windward (Atlantic) side of the islands can bring even richer rewards to the galley. Expect dorado, wahoo, yellowfin and blackfin tuna, barracuda, kingfish, Spanish mackerel, jacks and snapper. But we'll get back to such tropical exotica later – let's start with the basics.

Who said the Mediterranean is fished out? This albacore was caught between Menorca and Sardinia and fed the crews of several boats at the evening anchorage.

HANDLINES – THE BASIC INSHORE RIG

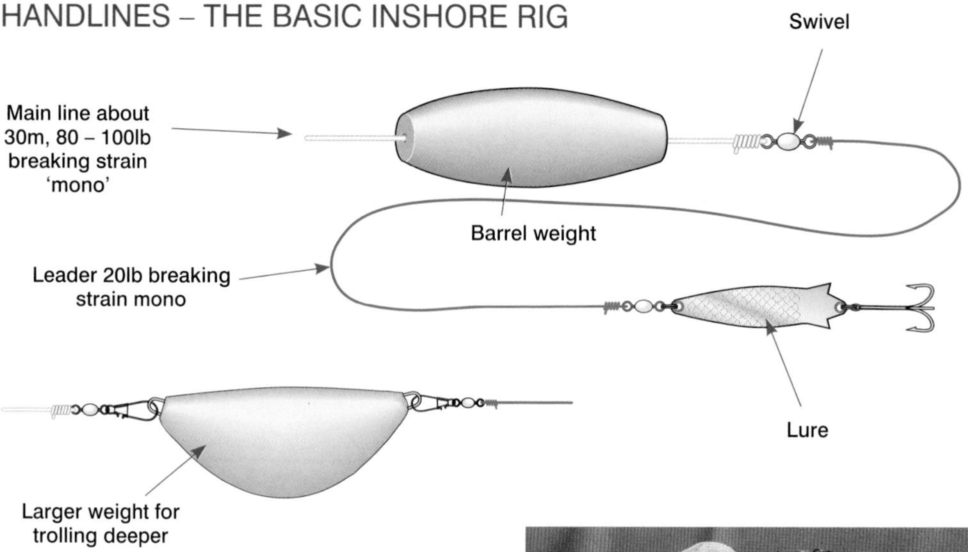

This homemade plywood lineholder has given over a decade of good service. Note the small plastic paravane, of which more later.

Very simple equipment will get you something for the grill pan at the lowest possible cost. About 30m of 80lb to 100lb (36 to 45kg) breaking strain monofilament (widely known as 'mono') or braided polyester (Dacron) main line, a sinker, a swivel, a less visible leader of 20lb (9kg) breaking strain mono and a suitable lure is all you'll need. The entire rig can be stowed on a plastic 'yo-yo' or a line holder, ready for immediate deployment. You can make a line holder very easily from a scrap of plywood but it's less convenient to use than a yo-yo (below). Drop the lure over the stern and hold the yo-yo so the line spills off freely. Once you've let out the required amount, take a few turns around a cleat or stanchion base to avoid losing the whole shebang. The sinker can either be of the barrel type sliding freely on the main line, or a fixed trolling weight attached between the main line and the leader. You're ready for action.

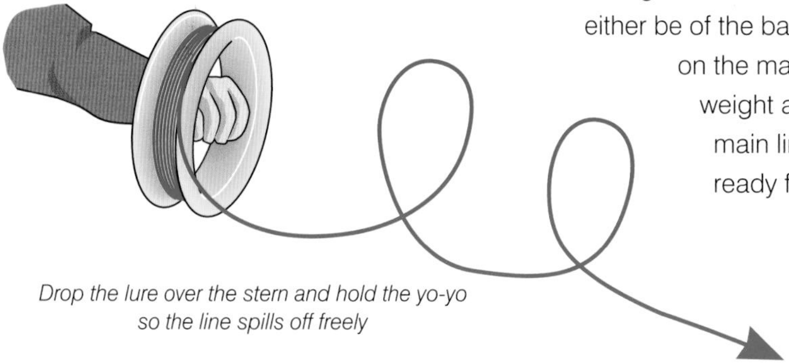
Drop the lure over the stern and hold the yo-yo so the line spills off freely

MACKEREL AND GARFISH

Mackerel and garfish, neither representing a threat to the other, often shoal up together in their hunt for brit – the small fry upon which they both feed. Brit, along with other panicked bait fish under attack, tend to swim towards the surface. Here, they receive the combined attention of birds from above and fish from below. A flawed escape strategy, maybe, but the resulting commotion is a sign of almost guaranteed success for us.

Perhaps, like me, you've childhood memories of jigging for mackerel with a string of gaudy feathers from a drifting boat. If you had lucked into a shoal, you would catch them by the bucketful. But if you hadn't – you wouldn't. When trolling, though, you have a good chance of stumbling across a series of shoals and picking up one or two fish from each as you sail through. The most productive speed is around 3 knots, but a determined individual of either species will manage to grab the lure at up to 5 knots or so. A large mackerel will be around 350mm long, and a small 'joey' mackerel around 150mm. Garfish average around 500mm long.

Any small lure that spins, wobbles or wriggles as it moves through the water is likely to deceive the humble mackerel. Even more so if it's also bright and shiny. Rather than leaving the rig to fish for itself, try jerking the line by hand from time to time. This will bring more life to the lure and imitate the darting back and forth of a small fish. You will also know immediately when you've hooked a fish, and are therefore less likely to lose it. One particular lure is indelibly associated with mackerel – the unimaginatively named 'mackerel spinner'– but other small spinners are equally as effective.

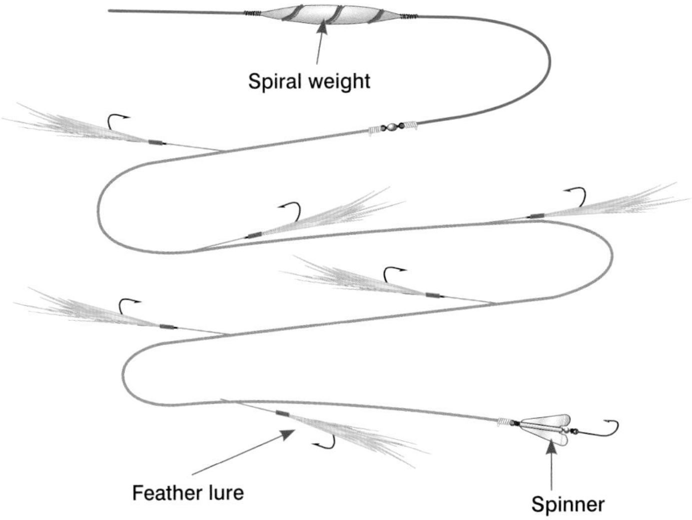

Spinners are small metal lures which can be either trolled or cast by rod and line (see page 69).

Their component parts are a wire shaft around which a metal blade rotates when drawn through the water. The body of the spinner is built up by coloured beads or shiny metal rings around the wire shaft. The blade is often polished and mirrored to reflect and transmit flashes of light as it spins around the shaft. A Mepps® spinner is a typical and well-proven example. The 'Aglia Glo' type have blades that are stimulated by ultra-violet light which continue to glow long after the other colours have disappeared, making them particularly suitable for low light conditions. You could also try a small polo spoon or a toby lure, both of which tend to wobble and wriggle rather than rotate.

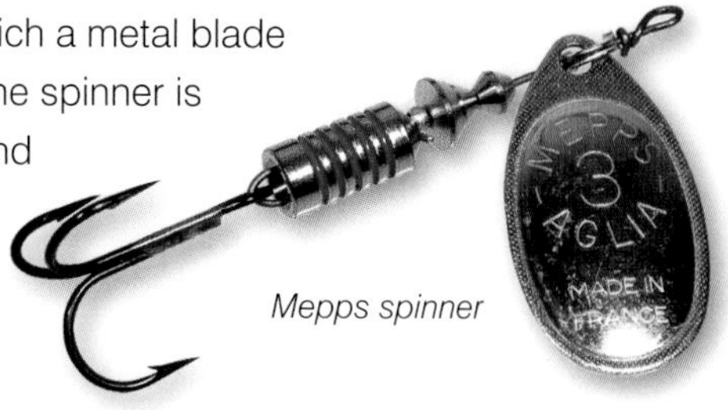

Mepps spinner

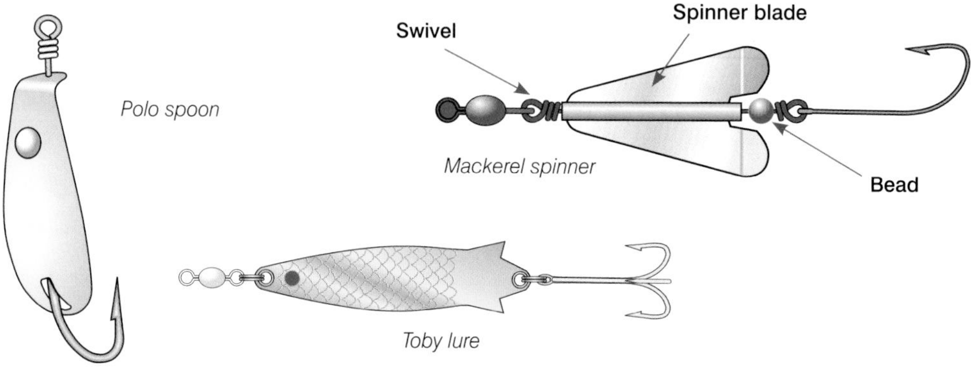

Polo spoon

Mackerel spinner

Toby lure

Having already named one manufacturer, it's worth mentioning that there are others whose products are not inferior in any way. But I have proved to myself that those products I have named are capable of doing what they're intended to do – catch fish!

Once you've caught a mackerel or a garfish you can, through a little butchery, add a silvery sliver of flesh to the hook. Leave the skin on and hook through the forward end, flesh side first, ensuring that the barb protrudes through the skin. This way, the flakes of the flesh will align with the water flow while the barb holds it in place, extending the useful life of the strip.

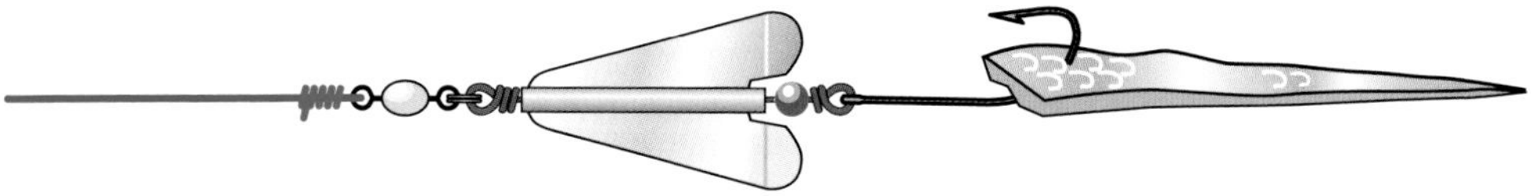

The strip must be thin in section and narrow in width or it will destroy the action of the lure. Properly rigged it will flutter around and leave a fishy trace in the water, bringing further allure to your lure.

At times the fish are feeding just below the surface, but often you'll find them deeper. Try to get your lure about 3m to 5m down by employing a lead sinker rigged not less than 4m ahead of the lure – and experiment from there.

Sinkers come in three types:

- **Drilled barrel leads and lead balls,**
- **Trolling weights, which have connection points at each end,**
- **Spiral leads, which can be fixed at any point by winding the line into the end springs and then around the spiral groove.**

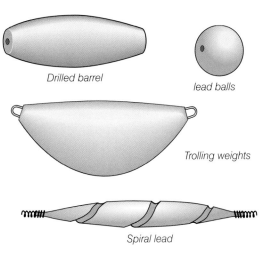

Drilled barrel

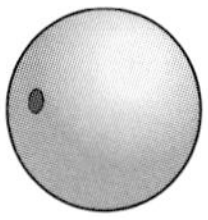

lead balls

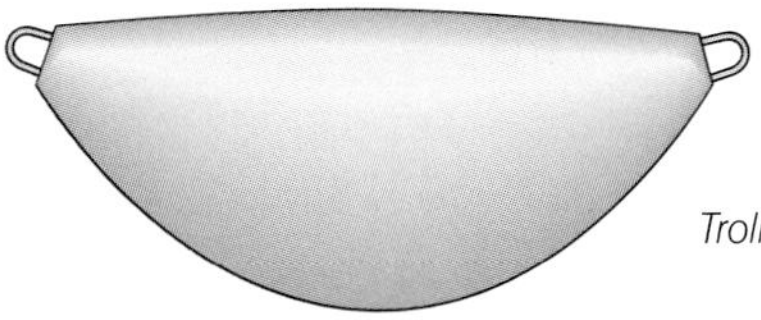

Trolling weights

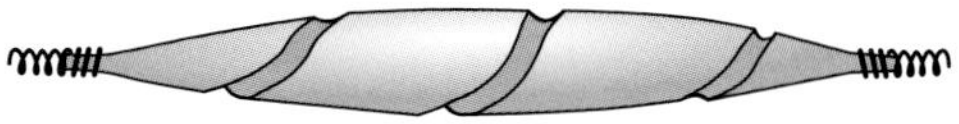

Spiral lead

The depth at which the lure settles is a function of the drag on the line, the weight of sinker and the speed of the yacht. Simply put, the faster you're sailing the heavier the sinker must be to maintain the same depth.

Making a lure

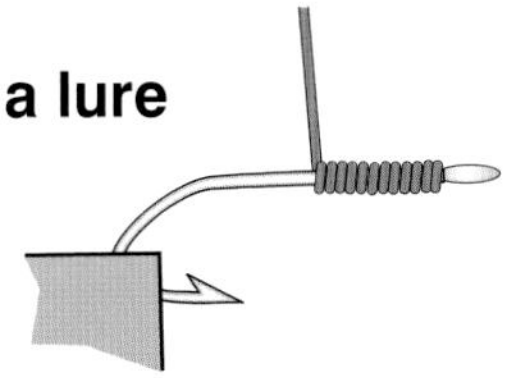

1. **With the hook in a small vice, pass the twine through the eye and whip about halfway down the shank, tucking the short end under the whipping.**

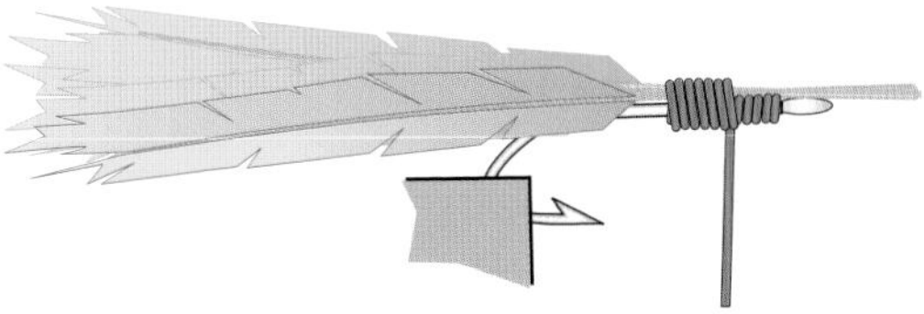

2. **Take a bunch of feathers and whip back towards the eye over their shafts.**

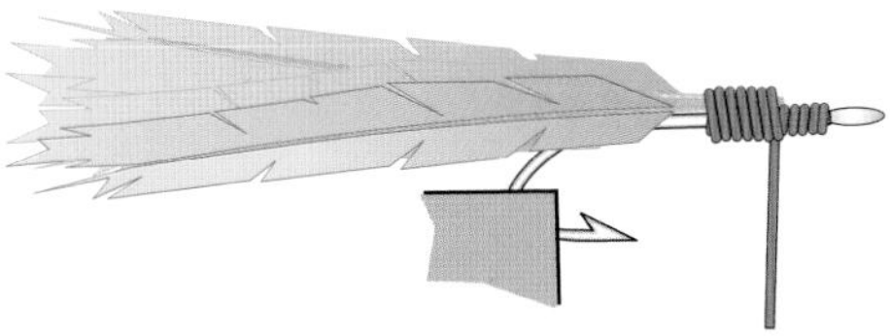

3. **Trim off the feather shafts with scissors of a scalpel. Be careful not to cut the whipping beneath. Then whip the rest of the way to the eye and ....**

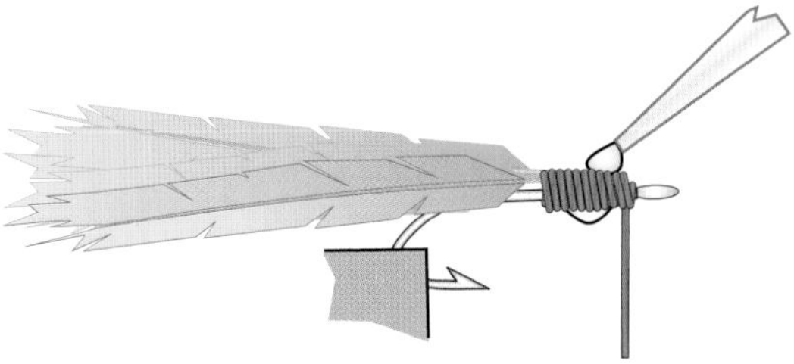

4. **.... cement the whole lot together with superglue, wiping off any surplus and maintaining tension on the twine until it sets.**

Finally, trim the feathers if necessary. If left too long the fish might not get the hook into its mouth. About 100mm will do nicely.

TIP Superglue can be used to attach the skirt but BE CAREFUL! It sticks skin as well as it sticks everything else – you might find yourself more attached to your lure than you would like.

PLANERS AND PARAVANES

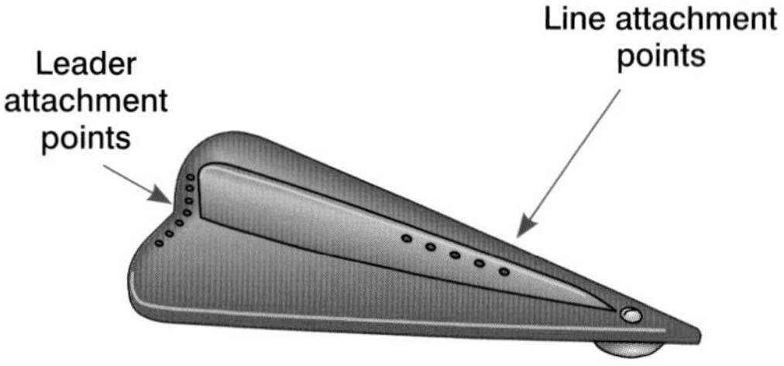

The opposite applies if you replace the sinker with a planer or a paravane (they mean the same thing). Made of either plastic or stainless steel, these devices work like an inverted wing, diving deeper as boat speed increases and dragging your lure down to a greater depth than it would otherwise achieve. The one illustrated here is a plastic model. They're attached between the main line and the leader, which should be around 7m long to prevent the turbulence created by the planer from spooking the fish. On some models, there's a choice of attachment positions, the furthest aft producing the steepest diving angle and vice versa. Most are ballasted by a moulded lead weight attached to the forward end and have the added benefit of capsizing when a fish strikes the lure, converting its 'dive' mode to 'climb', thereby bringing the fish to the surface.

But much more about planers later when we discuss trolling for the larger fish of the open ocean.

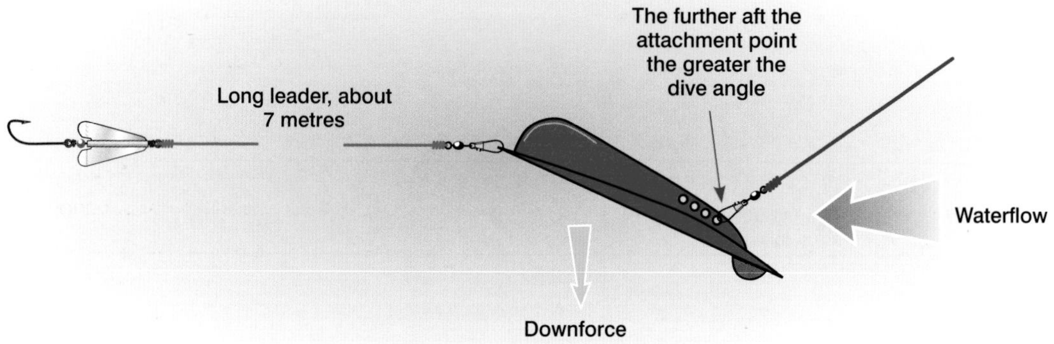

Made of either plastic or stainless steel, planers work like an inverted wing

THE UNI-KNOT: Although there are many alternatives, this simple knot is one of the most reliable methods of attaching line to such things as hooks, swivels and snap links. Unless otherwise noted, assume knots shown in these illustrations are the uni-knots. Instructions on how to tie both uni and and other useful knots, appear in the KNOTS section starting on page 81.

BASS

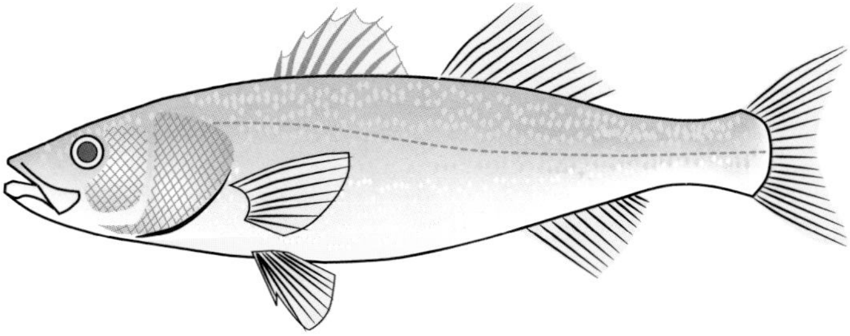

Bass are not as easy to catch as mackerel but are certainly worth the effort since they are considered to be one of the most delicious panfish to be caught

Unlike mackerel, which along with their tuna brethren are pelagic fish (though mackerel tend to stick fairly near coasts), bass prefer a more localised lifestyle. Typical habitats are offshore reefs, wrecks and sandbanks. So have another look at the chart. Are there any of these features on, or near, your planned route? If so, why not have a try for a bass? They're most likely to be dining on sand eels or small fish, so your lure should imitate either of these. An imitation sand eel, a 'Redgill' for example, would be a good choice. These rubber lures were developed over 30 years ago by Alex Ingram, and used with great success from his homeport, Mevagissey, on the south coast of Cornwall. Use the 150mm long version, together with a 4m long, 15lb (7kg) mono trace. Delta Eels and Eddystone Eels are two other similar artificials that, along with the Redgill, have a flat tail that gives them their characteristic waggling action. Bass hunt sand eels from below, where they're silhouetted against the light. It's not surprising then, that black or red frequently outperform all other colours.

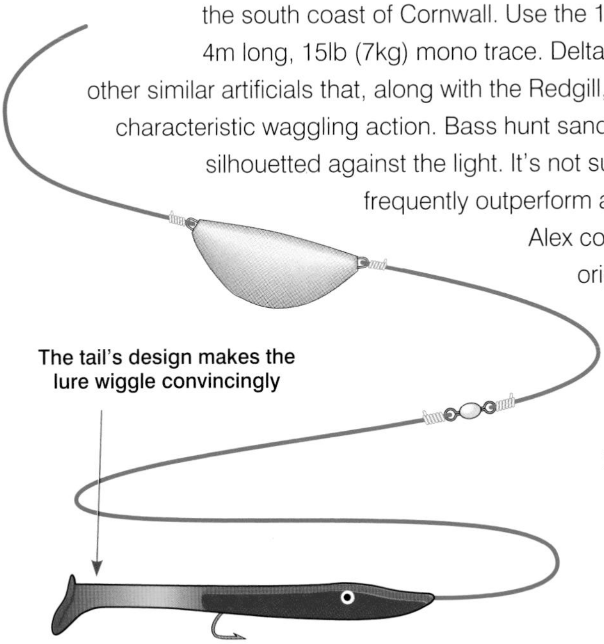

The tail's design makes the lure wiggle convincingly

Alex couldn't have imagined that his original design would be succeeded by the plethora of soft plastic-bodied lures that we can choose from today, and which are even softer and 'wrigglier' than his Redgill. Some are made of scent-impregnated soft plastic, even smelling like the real things! These are as close to a natural bait as it's possible to get, leaving a fishy trail behind them.

Although squid, shrimp, crabs and various other unlikely creatures are represented, these three types deserve a place in your tackle box:

- **Shads, which imitate small fish**
- **Jelly Worms, which imitate swimming marine worms such as ragworms**
- **Jelly Eels, which imitate sandeels.**

Probably the easiest way to use these is with a 'leadhead' which is a combined hook and weight. A barb at the back of the head ensures that the lure doesn't bunch up on the shank of the hook.

With some soft plastic lures you've the option of using them without a leadhead, in which case you'll need a special cranked hook, which similarly ensures they are towed along by the head and don't slide down into the bend of the hook. Fished in this way, they'll need a trolling weight some distance up the line as in the illustrated sand eel rig, or a few split shot squeezed on the line close to the lure. The heavier leadheads however – the 90g 'Bass Assassin' for example – can be fished without additional weight, depending on trolling speed and target depth.

But whether you use a leadhead or a cranked hook it's absolutely essential that the lure is rigged symmetrically, with the hook emerging exactly on the centreline and in the vertical plane. Otherwise, the lure won't swim convincingly and your chances of catching will be close to zero. Some shads are produced ready rigged with hooks and integral weights. Whilst undoubtedly effective, I prefer those with replaceable bodies. These are relatively cheap, particularly when bought in bulk, and enable you to ring the changes in terms of colour, type and size in the most cost effective way. A favourite food of bass is a small mackerel – a 'joey'. Many plugs and soft plastic lures are designed to resemble these, both of which will perform well at the preferred trolling speed of 1 to 2 knots.

Rigging unweighted shads

Place the jig hook alongside the lure and mark the place on the centreline at which the hook-point should emerge. Then insert the hook in the top of the lure's 'head', and in a single movement thread the hook through the lure and out at the mark. If the lure is either stretched or bunched on the hook you've not got it right.

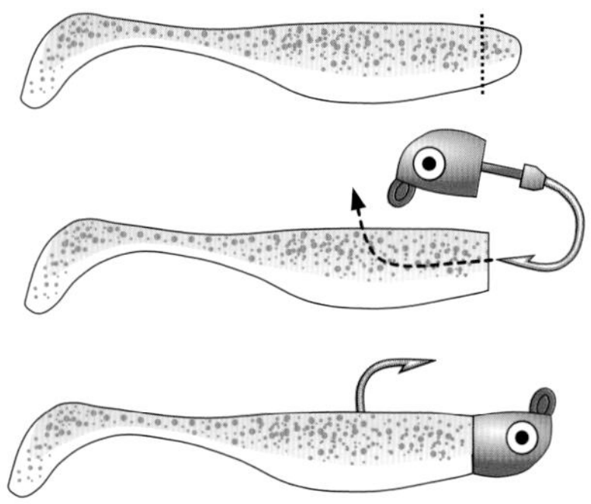

Rigging unweighted jelly worms

Insert a z-bend hook in the top of the lure's head and push it through. Feed the lure up to the eye of the hook and turn it so that the shank lies along the underside of the lure. Mark the point at which the hook point should be inserted on the underside, and where it should emerge on top – a few millimetres further aft – and push the point through so that the lure sits neatly in the bend of the hook.

And then there's the Dexter Wedge. This versatile lure comes in a number of sizes between 48mm (10gr) and 115mm (150gr). Designed primarily for casting, it also trolls well with a wobbling and flashing action and, in the larger sizes, it's a good jigging lure too (see page 59). You may be beginning to wonder if bass stand any chance at all.

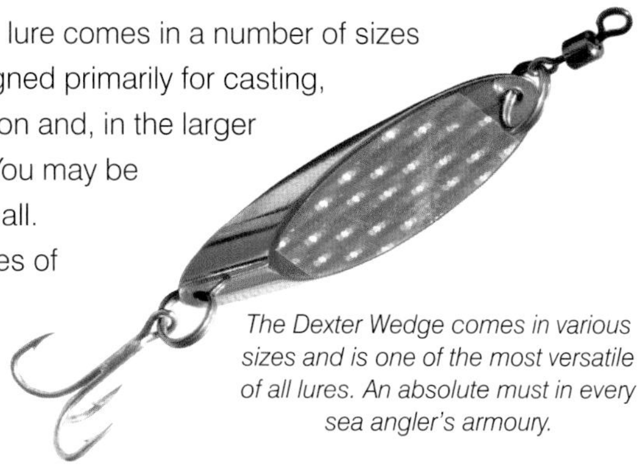

The Dexter Wedge comes in various sizes and is one of the most versatile of all lures. An absolute must in every sea angler's armoury.

Tiderips are favourite haunts of bass – examples of which in European waters include the Portland Race, the Alderney Race and the Raz du Seine. In these turbulent, oxygenated waters, professional bass fishermen operate powerful boats with great success. However, other than at slack water, most sailors will give these awesome places a wide berth – bass or no bass.

Bass are long-lived and slow growing. A fish of less than 360mm long, known as a 'school bass', is unlikely to have spawned and will be no more than 5 years old. Females can live for 30 years and reach 20lb in weight, but such fish are rare these days. Males seldom exceed 5lb. Currently, a minimum size limit of 375mm is imposed by law in UK waters, with smaller bass having to be returned to the water. Fish of this size can be lifted directly into the cockpit; for larger ones you will need a landing net. To avoid panicking the fish, sink the net below the surface and draw the fish into it rather than moving the net under the fish.

Pollack and coalfish share the bass's habitats and will also fall to your lure. They come a very poor second in terms of flavour though.

Attention to the following details will go a long way to ensuring a regular supply of good fish to your galley:

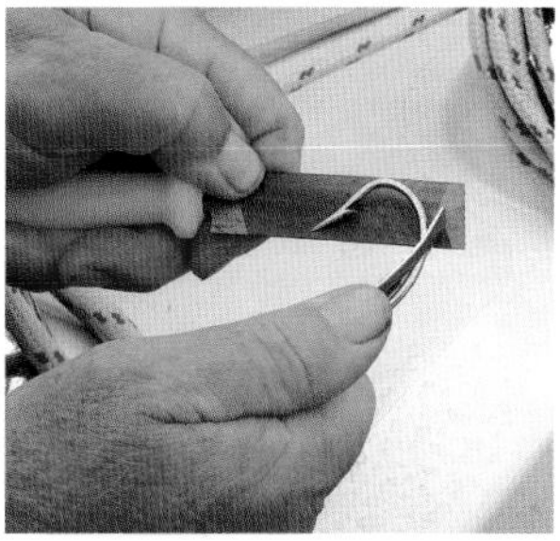

- **Use hooks of an appropriate size and keep them sharp.**
- **Learn the best knot for each particular application, and tie it with care.**
- **Learn your intended quarry's dietary preferences, and select a lure that imitates it.**
- **Experiment with the depth of the lure until you find where the fish are.**
- **Check the lure regularly and clear any seaweed or flotsam.**
- **Look for charted features such as changes in the seabed profile, reefs and currents where fish are likely to congregate.**
- **Look for signs of feeding fish such as bird activity on the surface of the sea. If you're prepared to alter course to intercept the fish below them you'll very likely be rewarded.**
- **Match the strength of any swivels to that of the line to which it's tied, and avoid weak links in your rig generally.**

AN OFFSHORE HANDLINE

The rig described for inshore waters is fine for smaller fish, but if you venture offshore a 'big-un' will one day deprive you of it. It must be scaled up.

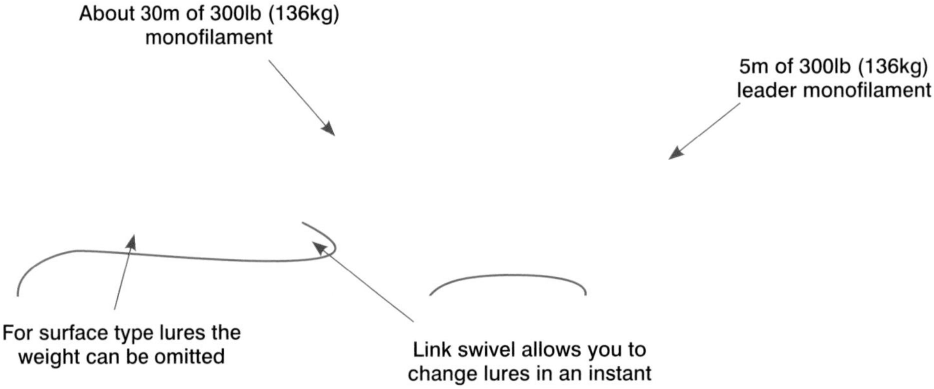

TIP
Silver swivels can attract the attention of fish in much the same way as a small lure would. To avoid the risk of having them bitten off, use black swivels.

Your offshore handline should consist of about 30m of 300lb main line, an optional lead sinker or planer, a heavy-duty swivel to prevent twists (this will also stop the sinker sliding down to the lure), a 300lb mono leader and a single lure imitating either a baitfish or a squid. Delicate it isn't.

The main line can be either mono or braided polyester, but both are subject to ultraviolet degradation and should be replaced periodically.

Crimps are used to make connections on mono line of this diameter, as it's difficult to cinch knots up tight on anything more than about 150lb. Your tackle shop might do it for you, but you'd be wise to invest in a crimping tool of your own. In the meantime resist the temptation to use parallel-jawed pliers which don't work well and can damage the line.

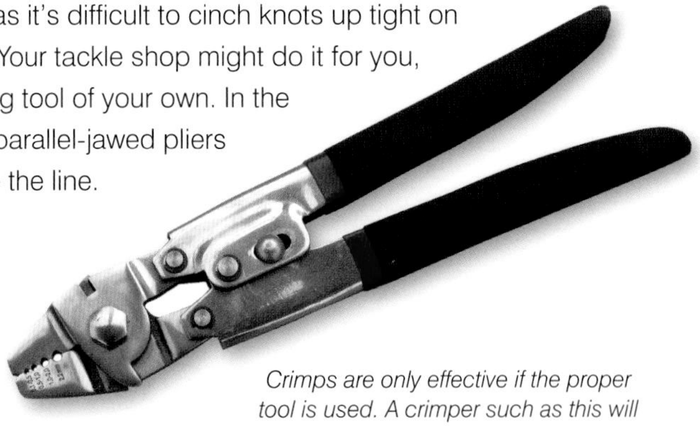

Crimps are only effective if the proper tool is used. A crimper such as this will serve for all common sizes.

SHOCK ABSORBERS

A large offshore fish is extremely powerful, and will hit your lure with surprising force, potentially enough to part your rig or rip the hook from its mouth. Some means of absorbing this impact load and the power of the fish's first run must be devised, or you're likely to lose your fish in the first few seconds.

It's not difficult to understand how it happens. When a large fish snaps up one of its smaller brethren, it rightly expects it to stop swimming. However, if the small fish is a lure firmly attached to a boat sailing at 6 knots, then its failure to stop will come as something of a surprise to the predator. A tuna can swim at 40-odd knots, and is very likely to do so once it discovers a fish with greater pulling power than itself. Exit one tuna, with or without lure, depending on where the weak point in your rig is. On a sailing boat, one way of absorbing this initial impact is to wrap several turns of line the 'wrong way' around a suitably positioned winch. There must of course be slack line between the winch and the point at which the line is secured to the boat.

This method gives an audible warning of a hooked fish, and is guaranteed to alert the most somnolent crew. The winch can then be used to retrieve the fish.

Another way of creating a shock absorber is to make up a snubber from a length of bungee cord, or other stretchy material. An added benefit of using a snubber is that its constant stretching and relaxing causes the lure to dart around realistically.

Snubber

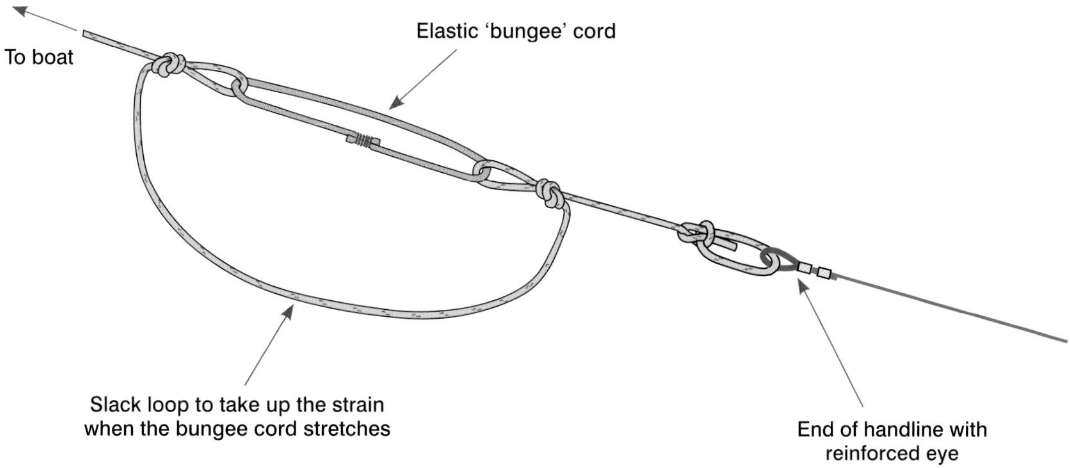

CAUTION: please don't use bungee cords with metal hooks on the ends. These are perfectly designed for the removal of eyeballs and, in my view, have no place on any boat.

LEADERS

It's best to use leader mono specifically manufactured for the job – namely, made of a material much harder than 'ordinary' mono of similar diameter. Most fish will have a problem with munching through a 300lb (136kg) mono leader of this type, but a hefty wahoo or a barracuda could manage it. So, to increase the odds of hanging on to their expensive lures, many anglers incorporate a short length of wire at the end of the leader, using a swivel to make the connection. To avoid having to handle the wire hauling your catch to the transom, it should be no longer than about 1.5m. It can be either single strand or multi-strand cable but shouldn't be of lower breaking strain than your main line. 7-strand cable is plastic sheathed, which makes it easier to work with but has an inherent susceptibility. Once the nylon is damaged – inevitable at the crimped connections – water creeps under the sheathing and corrodes the wire strand by strand. Expect to replace such leaders regularly.

Heavier 49-strand cable (manufactured by twisting together seven 7-strand cables) is uncoated and the most durable of all, but it's very conspicuous so can discourage fish.

Alternatively you could use single-strand wire which is certainly less visible, but is subject to metal fatigue after a while. This occurs particularly when using plugs that have a vigorous swimming motion, which will tend to bend the wire back and forth at the connection at the head of the lure. There are four types of single-strand wire available – tinned or galvanised wire (also known as music or piano wire), stainless steel, monel and titanium. My recommendation is to use monel wire, for the reasons set out in the table opposite.

Crimps won't hold in single-strand wire – you'll need to learn the Albright Special knot for joining it to your main line, and the haywire twist for the connection at the lure. (See knots section, starting page 81)

TIP **Always wear heavy gloves when hauling in a fish, or you risk serious injury to your hands. And never ever wrap the line around your hand. Even if the fish is small, a larger one may grab it, with dire consequences for your hand if you can't immediately let go. Haul the line in palms down so it would be pulled downwards from your grasp if there's a sudden surge. Have a knife readily to hand to cut the line if necessary. You may hook a fish that's far too powerful or dangerous or you may have entangled some part of yourself in the line. In this situation the voluntary loss of your most expensive lure is cheap indeed.**

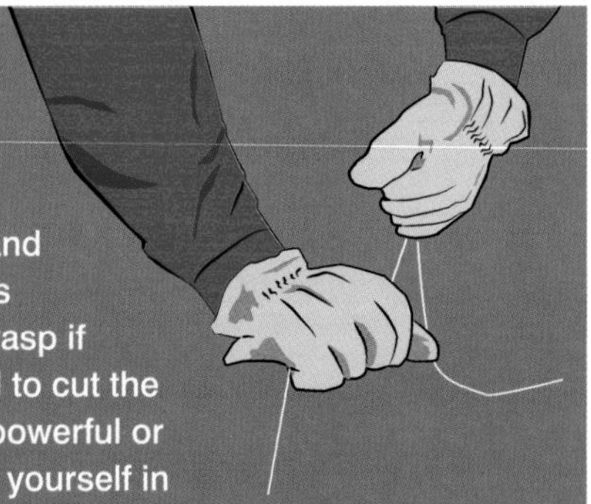

CAUTION: Don't be tempted to use the new generation very low stretch, small diameter braided lines as handlines as they can cut, even through gloves. These lines should only be used with a rod and reel, as discussed further on in this section.

The following table sets out the strengths and weaknesses of various leader materials

	STRENGTHS	WEAKNESSES
MONOFILAMENT		
Nylon	Inexpensive, supple, easy to knot or crimp	Poor resistance to teeth, large diameter compared to wire or cable of comparable strength
Fluorocarbon	Reputed to be virtually invisible under water, supple, easy to knot or crimp	Expensive, poor resistance to teeth, large diameter compared to wire or cable of comparable strength
SINGLE-STRAND WIRE		
Tinned wire (aka piano or music wire)	Inexpensive, resistant to sharp teeth, smaller diameter than monel or stainless for same strength	Subject to kinking, can only be connected by a haywire twist, not corrosion resistant so must be washed in fresh water after use
Stainless steel wire	Inexpensive, resistant to sharp teeth, small diameter, better corrosion resistance than tinned wire	Not very pliable and subject to kinking, can only be connected by a haywire twist
Monel wire	More pliable and less prone to kinking than stainless. Better corrosion resistance than stainless wire	Can only be connected by a haywire twist
Titanium wire	Flexible and kink resistant. Unequalled corrosion resistance and strength. Can be connected by Clinch and Albright knots	Expensive!
MULTI-STRAND CABLE		
Plastic coated (1x7)	Inexpensive, resistant to sharp teeth, more supple than single strand wire, easy to handle, easily joined with crimps, small diameter	More visible than mono or wire, coating susceptible to teeth or abrasive surfaces, undetected corrosion inside coating
Uncoated (7x7)	Resistant to sharp teeth, more supple than single strand wire, smaller diameter than mono of comparable strength, easily joined with crimps, very durable	More visible than mono or wire

TROLLING LURES

These are eminently collectable. I'm more likely to leave a bar without having a beer than to visit a tackle shop without buying a new lure. They fall into four main groups – skirted lures, spoons, plugs, and soft-plastic lures.

Skirted Lures

Skirted lures, designed to imitate squid and other cephalopods, should form the mainstay of your trolling arsenal. They are robust, effective and relatively cheap. Made up of three primary components – head, skirt and hook – they can be customised to suit a range of conditions and variety of species. The head is drilled through its centre and shaped to take a replaceable skirt. It's the design of the head that dictates the behaviour of the lure in the water, and most of the disturbance or 'noise' that's created as it's drawn along. The result of this disturbance is a stream of bubbles trailing behind the lure, and it's this so-called 'smoke trail' that's probably a skirted lure's most important attention-grabbing feature.

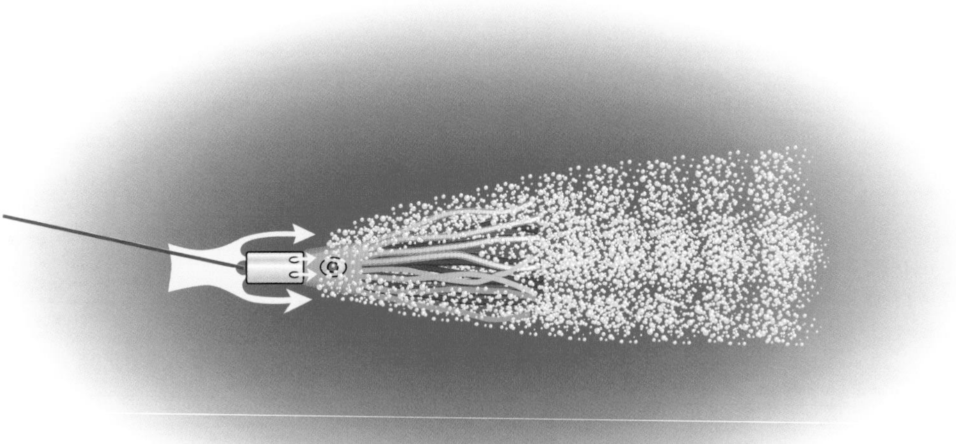

Jethead type lures attract attention to themselves by producing a stream of bubbles that look like a smoke trail

Inexpensive plastic skirts can be bought in a variety of styles and colours but you can make your own up even more cheaply. Strips cut from a plastic bag, feathers, fabric, silver foil, strands from a propylene rope – let your imagination and creativity loose.

The drag of the skirt stabilises the head and provides colour and bulk so as to create a squid-like silhouette for the fish to target. But for maximum attraction, the skirt should also contribute to the smoke trail through the inclusion of textured material in its construction. A popular skirt material for amateur lure makers is vinyl upholstery fabric, embossed on the topside with fabric backing on the other. So hang on to the off-cuts from your new cockpit cushions.

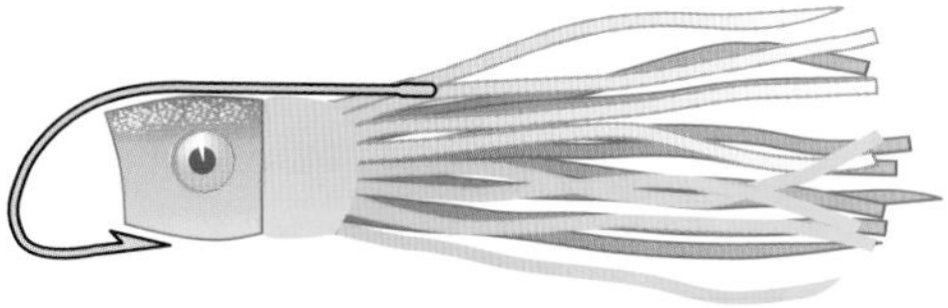

Use the lure head to gauge the correct hook size

The hook should be positioned such that it is only just concealed by the skirt – that is as far aft as possible, but not visible. The position is adjusted by adding beads on the line ahead of the hook. When selecting a hook for a skirted lure, the gape should be about the same as the maximum diameter of the lure head. If it's much smaller than this the head and skirt will mask the hookpoint and reduce hook-ups. Much larger and they will unbalance the lure and affect its action.

Replacing a skirt – first cut off the skirt, then...

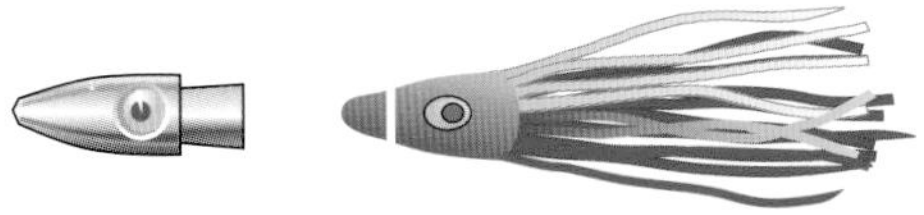

1. Cut the nose off the new skirt so it will just stretch over the lure head

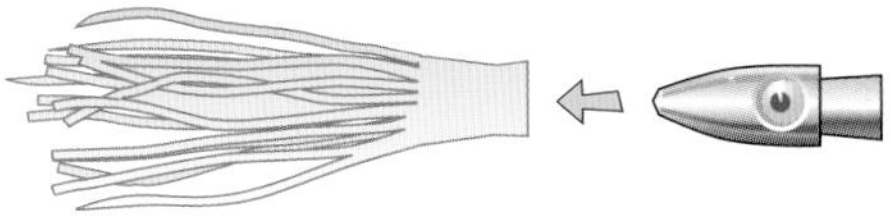

2. Turn the skirt inside-out and insert the lure head, front-end first, and push it to the end

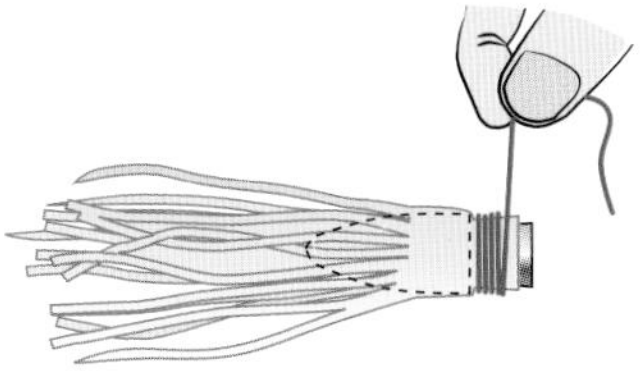

3. Bind the skirt with light line, nipping it tight in the necked section of the lure head

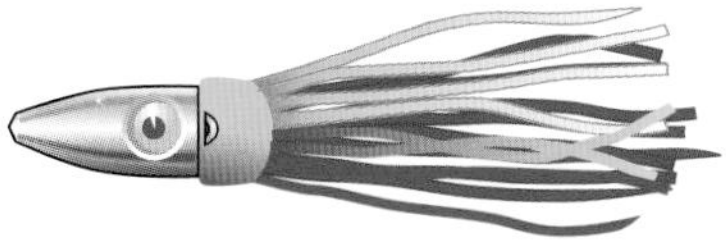

4. Roll the skirt back over the head, and there you have it – a virtually new lure! For a fuller or more colourful skirt, try a double

Head designs

Head designs fall into three main categories, each is best suited to a particular application:

BULLETHEADS: These are made of steel or chromed brass and, in reasonable conditions, run straight without much swerving and darting about. Smaller, lighter versions run close to and occasionally on the surface, creating a smoke trail, the intensity of which is proportional to the volume of water displaced by the lure head. The greater the diameter of the head, the wider and longer the smoke trail.

You'll find bulletheads with longitudinal holes drilled through them. These 'jetheads', as they are known, create an even better smoke trail, and are particularly attractive to tuna, dorado and wahoo – primary target fish when trolling in warm seas.

Bulletheads tend to get blown around in windy conditions, as their hydrodynamic shape doesn't give them much grip on the water. They lose effectiveness as a result.

FLATHEADS: Often made of alloy or plastic, these offer more resistance to the water and are a better choice in marginal conditions. Flatheads also track straight, occasionally breaking the surface, splashing and popping much like a flying-fish on their return from flight. Those with a tapered head hold the water particularly well. A derivation of a flathead is a 'chugger'. In these, the flat face has been hollowed out, giving them an even better grip on the water and a 'head-shaking' action. An obvious choice when the sea's getting up and you're starting to wonder if you ought to be fishing at all.

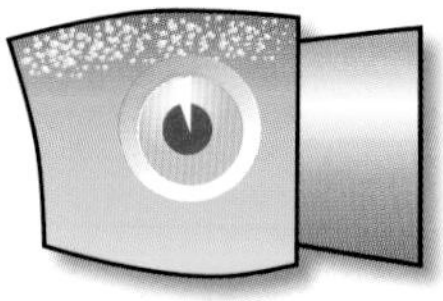

SLANT-HEADS (OR 'DIGGERS'): These come in two basic categories – pusherbaits and taperbaits – and, again, can be made of alloy or plastic. 'Pusher-baits' are at their best in gentler sea states. Also known as 'straight runners', these track on or just below the surface creating a deal of disturbance, as they dart from side to side. 'Tapers' have the slanted face but have an increasing diameter from front to back. These tend to run sub-surface most of the time, but occasionally break out much like a flathead. Just to complicate matters further, those with longer tapered heads are often known as 'plungers'. These have a more aggressive action and can be used effectively over a wide range of conditions.

The tuna feather

There's another type of lure that deserves a mention – the tuna feather. These have a weighted head and skirt made of feathers, and they don't just catch tuna. One of the largest barracuda I've ever caught was on one of these. We had just passed between Sister Rocks and Cistern Point, close to the anchorage at Tyrrell Bay at Carriacou in the West Indies, when the reel started its characteristic scream.

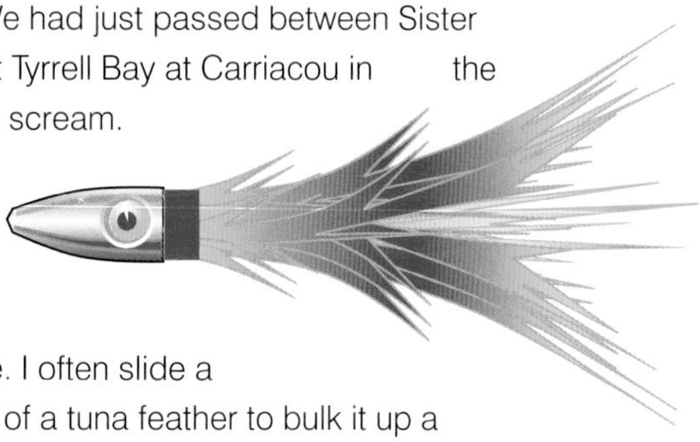

I'm not a fan of large barracuda, much preferring spanish mackerel, two of which were already in the cool box. The good people of Carriacou have no such hang-ups, and a call on the VHF soon had a grateful recipient alongside. I often slide a muppet (soft plastic imitation squid) over the head of a tuna feather to bulk it up a bit, and increase the smoke trail. If you decide to give this a try, select a muppet that will fit snugly over the head of the tuna feather and trim the plastic 'tentacles' such that they don't completely mask the feathers.

CAUTION: In big-game tackle shops you'll find some examples of skirted lures well over 300mm long. These are used for marlin and other giants I'd rather not mess with. Lures of 100mm to 200mm long are best for cruisers like us, just looking for something tasty for the pot.

TIP As shown on page 12 a strip of fish or squid added to the hook of your skirted lure or tuna feather will leave a scent trail in the water, and enhance your strike rate particularly at slower trolling speeds. Change it regularly, as its potency will be lost once the oils are washed out. The squid strip should be cut from the mantle and trimmed to a tapered shape. Hook through the thick end, allowing the tapered end to waggle around. Cut the fish strip longitudinally from the silvery flanks or belly, leaving the skin on. Trim it as for the squid, hooking through the forward end of the strip. This way, the flakes of the flesh will align with the water flow, extending the useful life of the strip.

Daisy Chains

A 'daisy chain' deserves a place in your lure bag. This is a string of three to five skirted lures or soft-plastic lures on a trace of around 2m to 3m long. It's designed to imitate a predatory fish chasing a shoal of smaller baitfish fleeing line-astern. Only the lure at the rear has a hook, the others acting solely as attractors. It's important that each lure in the daisy chain is identical, except for the chaser which can be larger and of a different appearance. Each skirted lure leaves an enticing trail of bubbles in the water, which may explain the 'fish killer' reputation of the daisy chain.

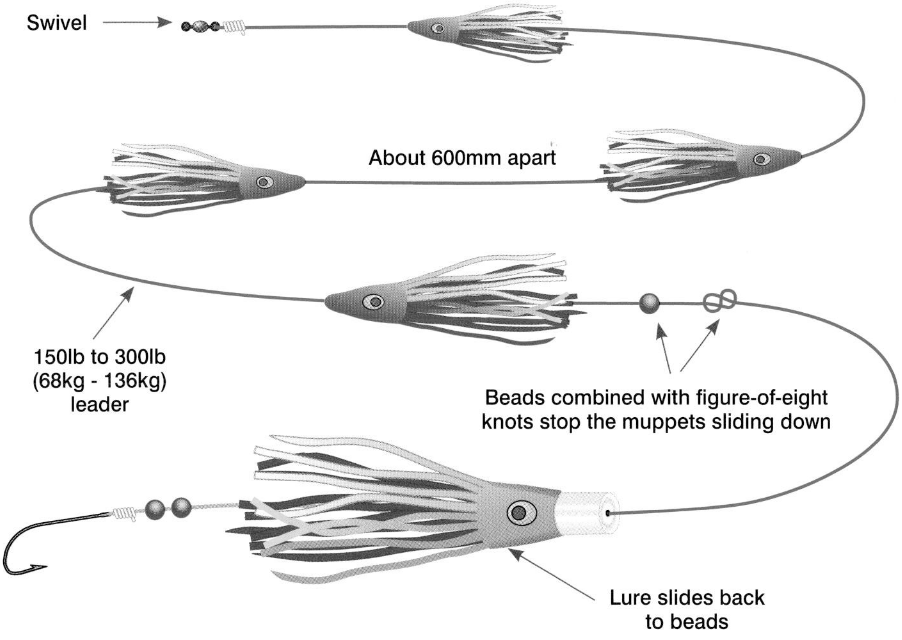

The daisy chain is a potent fish catcher. Note that only the rear-most lure has a hook.

Spoons

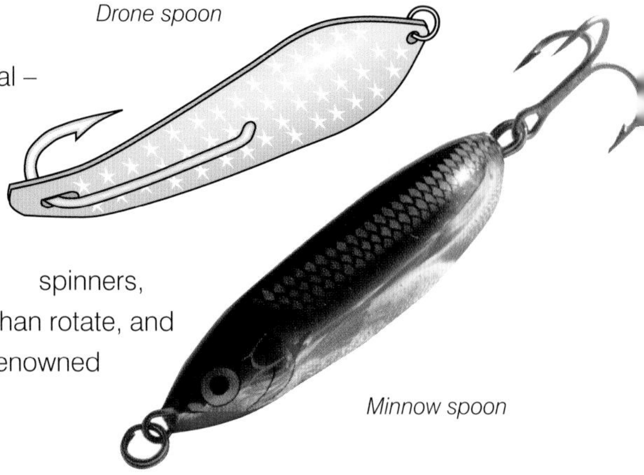

Spoons are pressed from a single piece of metal – most varieties being drilled at each end for a split ring. A swivel is attached at the front end and a hook – often a treble – at the other. Some are brightly coloured or chromed and others have a polished glittery surface. Unlike spinners, these are designed to wobble and flash rather than rotate, and range in size from 40mm to 150mm. They are renowned fish-catchers.

Other varieties though, Such as Drones, Clarkespoons and Luhr Jensen 'PET' spoons for example, have the hook attached rigidly to the spoon.

They're all best fished slow (ie 2kn or less) and well below the surface, often in conjunction with a downrigger as described on page 51.

Plugs

These are hard, moulded lures designed to imitate small swimming fish. Their bodies are commonly made from plastic or resin, or wood – either balsa or a hardwood such as beech – and usually come already fitted with hooks. There are two main types:

1. Surface plugs, which topple and splash around on the surface. These are most effective when trolled slowly in gentle seas. Characteristically they have blunt faces and no vanes. They're just the thing when the wind has fallen away and the sea has little more than a gentle ripple on its surface. Hits can be spectacular, with striking fish carrying the lure high into the air. At other times your lure will vanish in a gentle swirl.

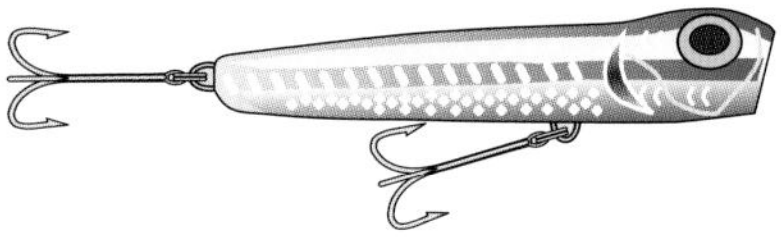
Surface plug

2. Swimming plugs operate below the surface at various depth ranges. When static, some float and others don't, but both types dive to a greater or lesser extent when pulled through the water. This diving ability is normally down to a metal or plastic vane at the nose of the lure, but other 'vibration' types achieve it through their body design. These types are characterised by a flat upper surface to their head, a deep body which gives them stability, a towing eye aft of the head and are weighted to achieve a 'nose-down' attitude. Their unique design forces water directly towards the upper forward part of the lure, pushing it downwards and causing it to wriggle energetically. The resulting vibrations invite the attention of interested parties over great distances.

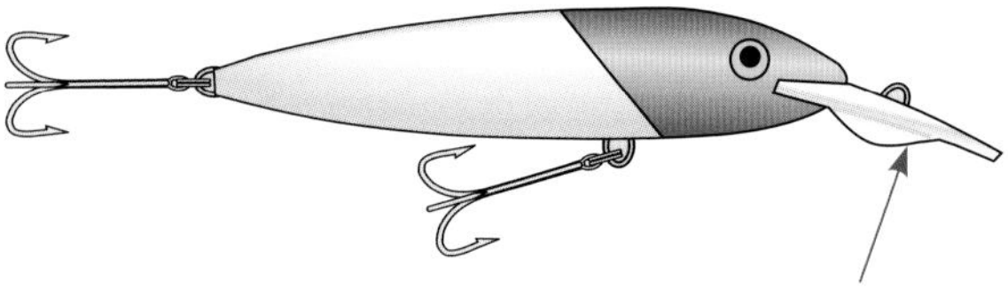

Swimming plug

The depth at which the vane types operate is dependent on the design of the vane – the closer the vane is to horizontal and the greater its surface area, the deeper the lure dives. Deep diving plugs can get to around 10m or so without the assistance of weights, planers or wire lines. If the lure has a shallow, almost vertical vane, you can be sure that it's a buoyant lure designed to operate close to the surface. Top manufacturers of these types of lures often print the performance characteristics on the packaging, so it's worth checking what it says on the box.

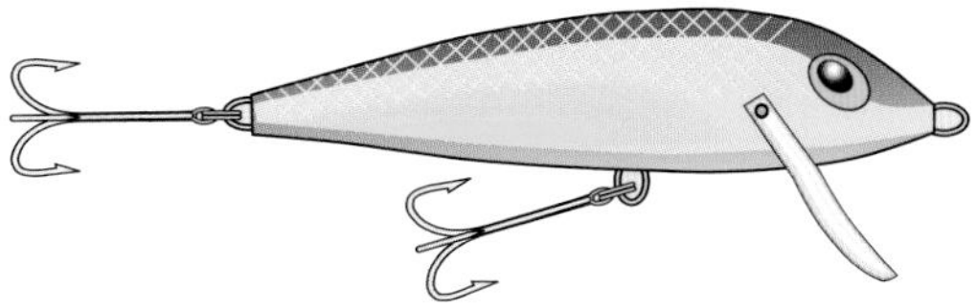

With its steeply inclined vane, you might think this lure would dive deep. In fact, the reverse is the case

Plugs with metal vanes need occasional adjustment as they can be knocked out of alignment, causing the lure to run erratically or capsize. Check their action regularly, and if the lure veers off to one side or the other, gently bend the nose ring to the same side. Continue to check and adjust until it runs straight and true, taking care not to over-adjust. Plugs with plastic vanes won't need adjustment.

Plugs are expensive in comparison to other types of lures of similar size – I've been accused of sulking for hours when I've lost one. Unfortunately, many of those on the market are of doubtful quality, with weak hooks, joints and leader attachment points. Good quality models have an internal continuous metal rod that connects the hooks directly to the leader attachment point.

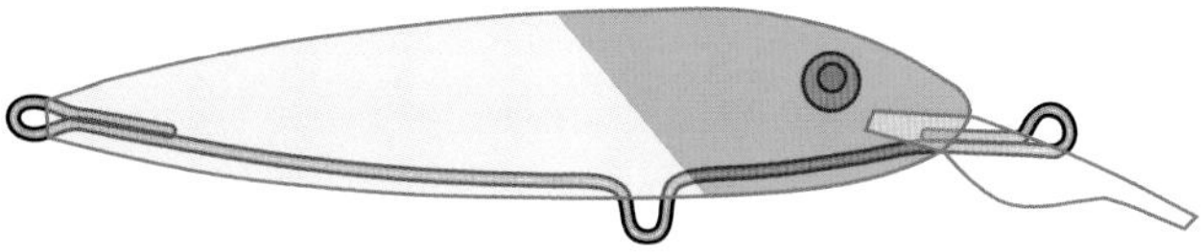

The best quality lures have an internal wire so their bodies play no part in maintaining the strength of the rig

Most plugs sport a pair of treble hooks. Although this would seem to offer the best chance of hooking up, many anglers are convinced that the third hook on a treble can sometimes lever the hook from the fish's mouth during the fight. They therefore replace the trebles with double hooks. Undoubtedly doubles are stronger than trebles, but if you choose to change them, check that this doesn't spoil the lure's swimming action, rendering it less effective. If it does, change back.

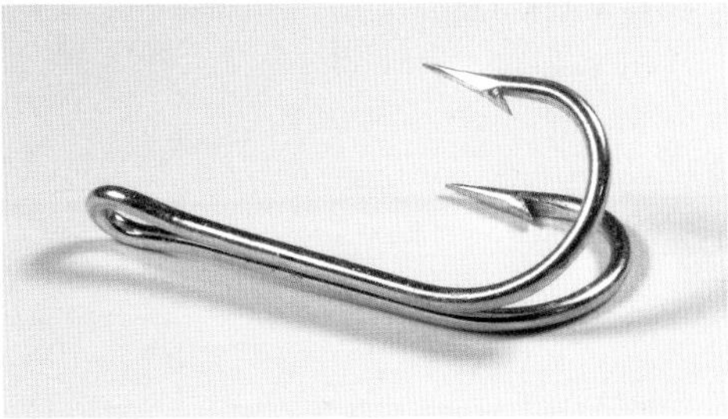

A double hook

TIP **If, despite all precautions, twists develop, remove your rig and trail all of your line astern to allow it to unwind.**

Some hollow plugs contain beads. As well as adding weight, these rattle around inside and transmit vibrations which are picked up by the pressure sensitive cells in the fish, enticing it to investigate. Others have holographic bodies and 3D eyes. Fish detect their food through vibration, scent and vision, so anything you can do to stimulate their sensory receptors is worth a try.

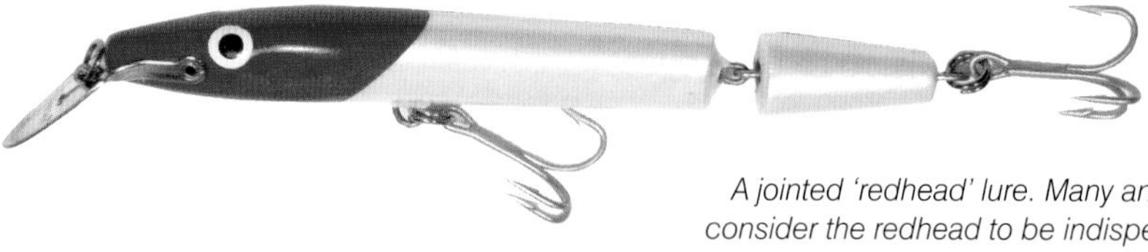

A jointed 'redhead' lure. Many anglers consider the redhead to be indispensible.

Many big-game fishermen will tell you if you have only one lure on board it should be a 'Red-Head' plug. This design is reputed to have caught every type of gamefish in all of the world's oceans at some time or other. Jointed plugs have a particularly lifelike swimming action, but whether or not they catch more fish than unjointed ones is debatable. Each type has its supporters, but I remain an agnostic on this one. Jointed or otherwise, when a fish grabs one it will quickly realise its mistake and try to get rid of it in a hurry. So unless the hooks have taken an immediate and secure hold you'll lose your fish, which is one reason why soft-plastic swimming lures were developed.

Soft-plastic swimming lures

On taking one of these, your fish believes he's got hold of the real thing, and is more likely to munch merrily away for a while, giving you more time to set the hook. Smaller lure sizes, such as the shads mentioned earlier for bass, work well at slower trolling speeds and will catch smaller pan-size fish, but for larger offshore species and higher trolling speeds you'll need larger lures. The 'Live Series' lures made by Williamson Lures are very good, and are said to equal the effectiveness of natural bait. They're made in various sizes up to an enormous 450mm ribbonfish designed to dupe the largest gamefish, but one of their smaller squid or ballyhoo lures would be about right for a catch of more appropriate size. As mentioned earlier, they're very realistic, both in appearance and to the touch, and swim in a most convincing manner when trolled at between 3 knots and 8 knots. But they are expensive, and durability isn't one of their selling points. Whilst you can catch several dorado or tuna before the lure is destroyed, a single strike from a wahoo and it's likely to be game-over.

An imitation plastic mackerel – effective but easily damaged

Storing your Lures

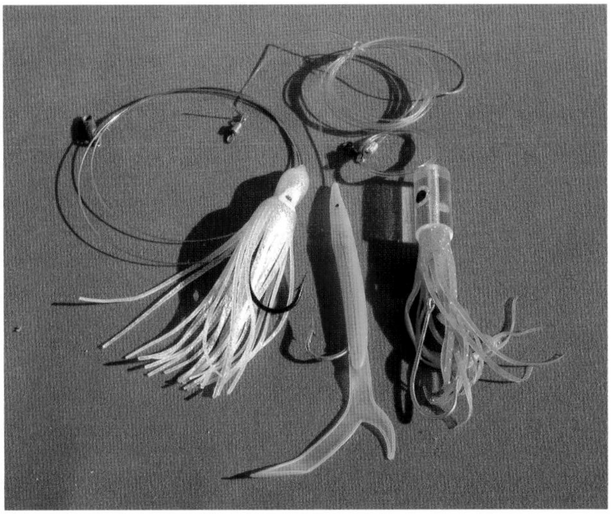

It's dangerous to leave your lures lying about. If you store them together in a box, particularly with leaders attached, a fine old tangle will result. It's far better to store them in lure bags, which will eliminate tangles, protect the hook points and delay the fading of coloured skirts. Before stowing them away after a day's fishing, swill them off in fresh water to remove the salt. Once they've dried, a quick squirt of moisture repellent lubricant on the swivels and hooks will help keep corrosion at bay.

The ideal lure bag should have a breathable vinyl back – in case the lures aren't quite dry when you put them away – and a clear front, so you can see what's inside. Coil the leaders and store one lure to a bag. The bags can be made up singly, or in a series of up to about five or so.

Hooks, other than those made of stainless steel, corrode remarkably quickly in seawater. Even after a day's use, your carefully honed hook point will become blunt through corrosion. But a dab of lanolin on the point will protect it and keep it sharp. Lanolin is a wax processed from sheep's wool and can be bought from pharmacists' stores.

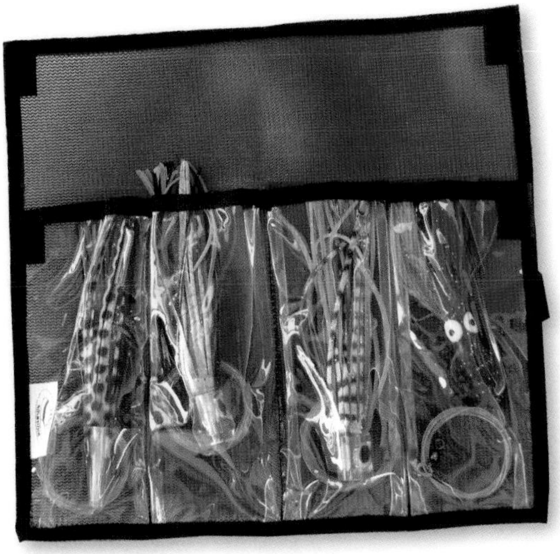

The ideal lure bag should have a breathable vinyl back and a clear front, so you can see what's inside.

Take care when handling lures. It's very easy to get a hook embedded in your finger, even if there's no fish involved. The risk is reduced by protecting the hook points whenever it's practical. Use corks or polystyrene foam for single and double hooks, and proprietary plastic protectors for small treble hooks. Alternatively a short piece of plastic tube can be pushed over the point and barb. Don't try to remove a lure from a large fish before it's properly subdued, and even then use long-handled pliers or a proprietary hook extractor designed for the purpose.

HOOKED ON FISHING

If, despite these precautions, you or a crew member is unlucky enough to get impaled on a hook, one of the following methods will get it out.

First, clean around the point of entry with antiseptic ointment. If the hook has entered in such a way that the point is close to the skin, you should consider the 'push and cut' method:

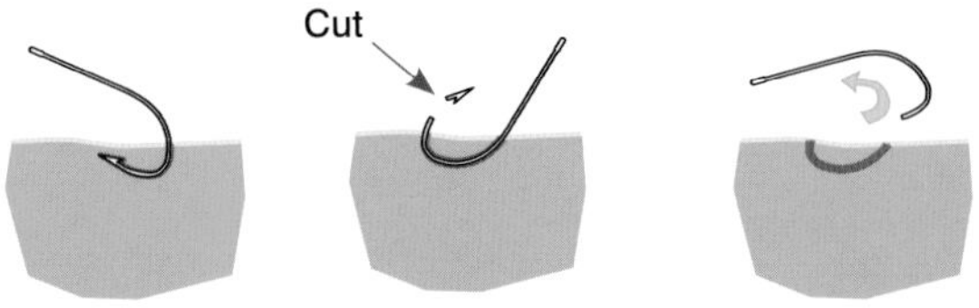

1. **Push the hook through so that the point and the barb exit the skin**
2. **Cut off the point below the barb with a pair of pliers**
3. **Withdraw the hook in the direction from whence it came.**

A disadvantage of this method is that it's quite painful and creates a further wound. A less painful alternative, and the one to use where the hook point has not gone in so far is the 'snatch method':

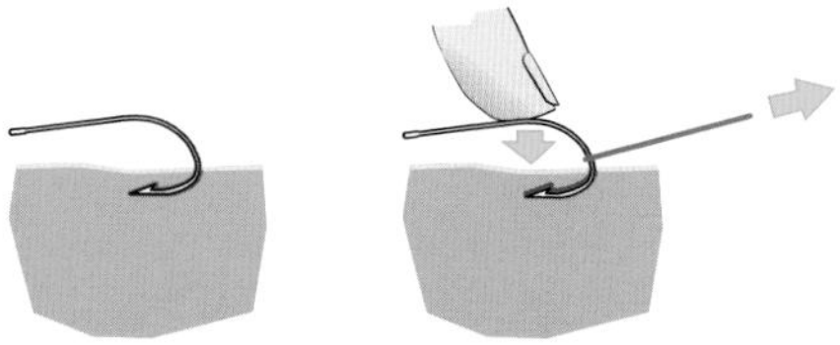

1. **Loop a length of line of not less than 20lb breaking strain around the bend of the hook**
2. **Get a firm grip on the line, by wrapping it around your hand**
3. **With your other hand, press the eye of the hook down towards the surface of the skin and back toward the hook's bend, as if trying to back the hook out along the path of entry. This will disengage the barb from the flesh, and align the embedded part for removal**
4. **While pressing on the hook eye, give the line a short, sharp pull parallel to the skin and in line with the hook, to snap the hook back out of the wound.**

Whichever method you use, always wash the wound thoroughly, apply antiseptic ointment and a simple dressing. Check that your tetanus shots are up to date, and if not, attend to it at the earliest opportunity.

Be particularly careful when removing a multi-hooked lure. I met a French skipper in Martinique who, while attempting to remove a treble hook from his crew's hand, managed to impale his own finger on a second treble on the same lure. Being in mid-Atlantic at the time, the prospect of sharing each others' intimate moments for 1,500 miles was not a cause for celebration. In future, he told me, he would either remove, cut off the points, or tape up all other hooks before attempting first aid.

TROLLING SPEED

Few, if any, cruising sailboats are capable of sailing quickly enough to outrun blue-water game fish, thereby avoiding catching them. Although 6 knots or so is the maximum speed you can reasonably expect to catch a bass, charter trolling boats often fish at 12 knots or more for pelagic gamefish. On 'Alacazam' we bring our lines in when our speed reaches 8 knots or so.

Any faster, and we would prefer not to have to deal with an underwater rocket wanting to go the other way. A good fish will be halfway to the horizon before you've reduced sail and slowed the boat down sufficiently to start bringing him in.

Most lures are designed for optimum performance within a specific speed range, so it's important not to purchase a lure whose optimum performance exceeds your maximum speed. In the absence of any advice on the lure packaging, your tackle dealer will be able to advise on this when you're buying the lure.

Trolling distance

Some sailors advocate trolling the lure about 100m astern of the boat, unwittingly placing the lure well aft of any fish drawn by their curiosity to the source of the major disturbance in the water. When trolling a single line, we normally place the lure between 15m and 30m aft of the boat, starting close to the surface, where a fish swimming below will see it silhouetted against the sky.

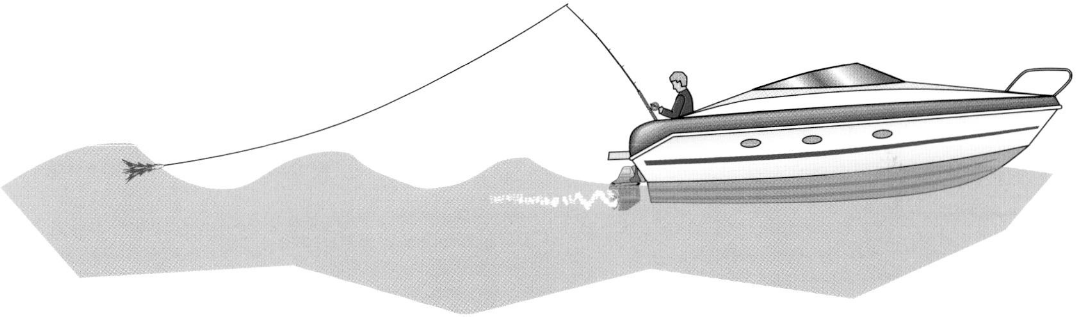

Powerboats generate standing waves in their wakes. About the third wave face astern is a good place to have your lure.

Although not a hard and fast rule, fish seem to feed close to the surface at dawn and dusk, and also on overcast days. Shoals of flying fish erupting from the surface are a clear indicator of when your lure should be fished shallow. If your lure breaks the surface now and again, it's no bad thing and can sometimes prove irresistible, particularly to dorado. At other times the lure should be fished deeper. A lead sinker will get a skirted lure a short way below the surface, but to reach fish at greater depths you'll need a deep-diving plug or a downrigger or a wire line rig as described later in this section.

TEASERS

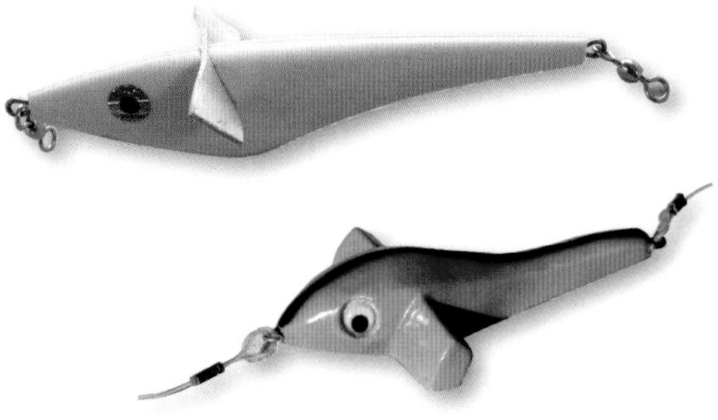

Pretty but otherwise harmless. Teasers (or birds) are the seducers of the fishing scene.

However attractive your lure, it won't catch fish if they don't know it's there. Teasers will help. These decoys mimic the disturbance made on the surface by a shoal of baitfish and, in doing so, attract predatory fish to the vicinity of your lure. An imitation flying fish known as a 'bird' is one such teaser. Attach it about 3m ahead of your lure, where it will splash around on the surface apparently under hot pursuit by your lure.

For even greater attraction you could attach your teaser ahead of a daisy chain.

Spreader bars deploy a number of teasers, creating a small shoal of hook-less skirted lures. These are normally made of stainless steel, but a cheap and cheerful spreader can be made from a plastic coat hanger and a few corks.

Teasers don't have to be attached to your main line, nor do they need to be of proprietary manufacture. Pretty much anything that floats and splashes about will do – a net bag filled with corks, a partially filled plastic bottle, a crushed beer can or a short length of wood perhaps. Improvise.

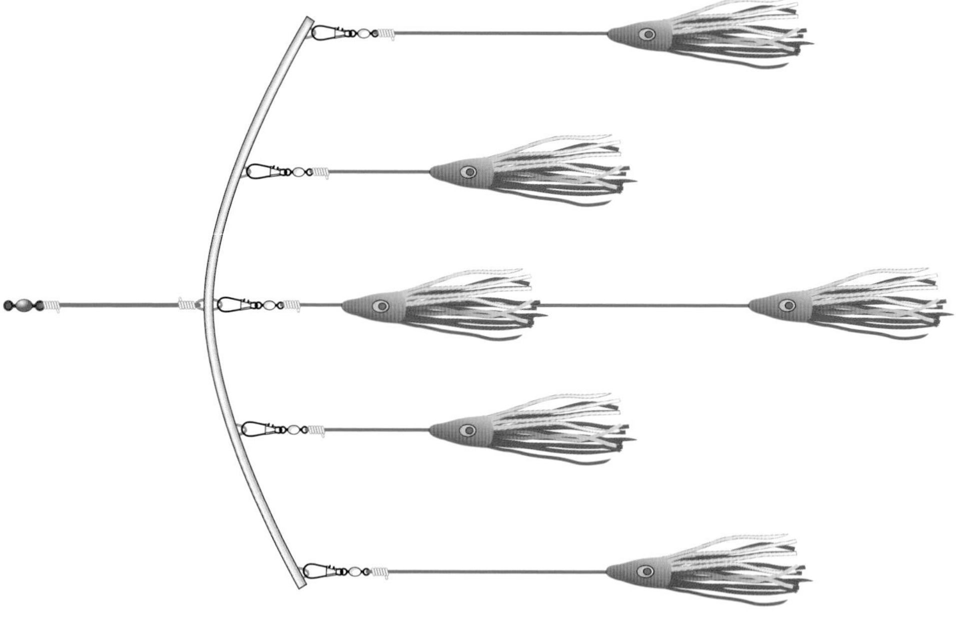

Not really for the occasional angler, a combination of a spreader bar and a shoal of muppets will soon have the fish taking notice.

NATURAL BAITS

A properly presented natural bait is second to none, not least because of the scent trail it leaves. Fresh squid, herrings, sardines and halfbeaks (or ballyhoo as they're known by most fishermen) should last two or three days if you can find space in the fridge. But if they're going to compete for martyrdom successfully with their living brethren, natural baits must 'swim' convincingly – they should wriggle, but not spin.

For a lifelike wriggle, the bait must be flexible, so the first steps in rigging a dead baitfish are:

- **Empty the bait's gut cavity by squeezing firmly with thumb and forefinger along the belly towards its anal vent, then...**
- **Pinch the bait progressively along its backbone to detach the flesh from the bone, but take care not to break the skin. Flex it back and forth a few times to complete the loosening up process.**

Spin avoidance is achieved by ensuring that the bait is symmetrical when viewed from head-on. The next steps are:

- **Remove the eyes. Otherwise water pressure may cause them to bulge unequally, inducing rotation. A small wooden dowel is ideal for pushing them out of their sockets.**
- **Trim off the pectoral and pelvic fins. Any unequal projection here and a propeller effect will be set up.**

When rigging the bait, great care must be taken to avoid destroying the symmetry. In particular:

- **The hook must emerge from the underside of the bait exactly on the centreline and in the vertical plane, and**
- **The fish must be towed by its head, leaving all parts abaft to wriggle naturally. If the towing load is allowed to shift to the bend of the hook, the bait will bunch up and lose any semblance of symmetry, becoming little more than a source of passing amusement to any potential customers.**

Properly executed, the following rigging techniques will achieve these essential objectives. Let's start with a small fish such as a sardine or joey mackerel.

Sardine (or similar)

First you'll need to decide on the leader material. Mono will allow the bait to work most convincingly, and will get the most hits as a result. But if you think a wahoo or some other toothy fellow may put in an appearance, wire would be a better choice. Use plastic covered seven-strand wire, as single strand wire doesn't lend itself to this technique. To get the hook in the right place, you'll need a baiting (or rigging) needle. This is a length of stainless wire, around 250mm long with a point on one end and an open eye at the other.

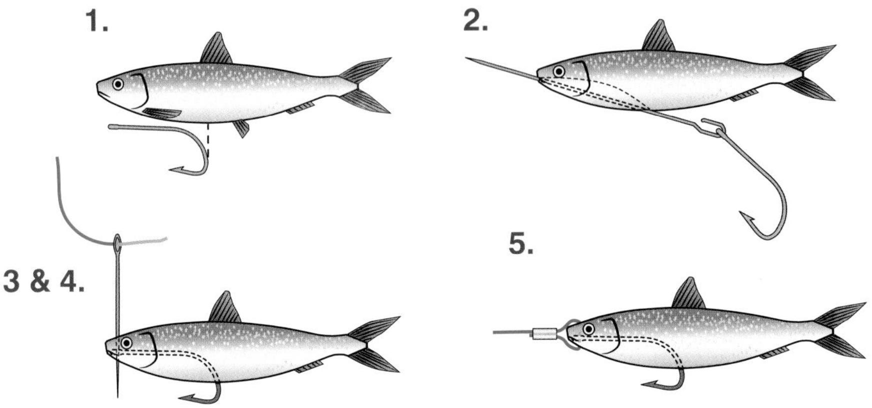

1. **Select a large hook, about one third the length of the bait. Use the point to mark the point, exactly on the centreline of the bait's underside, at which the hook will emerge. Then attach it to a hook type baiting needle.**
2. **Insert the baiting needle and push it through so it exits the fish's mouth. Pull the hook into the fish so it ends up in the position shown in 3. Detach the baiting needle.**
3. **Pull the hook into the bait's mouth and detach the needle.**
4. **Slide a crimp onto your leader, attach an eye type baiting and push the needle through the bait's head on the centreline, through the eye of the hook and out vertically below the point of entry.**
5. **Pull the end of the leader through and into the crimp, slide the crimp back close to the mouth and nip off the excess line.**

Eyeball the bait head-on. The hook and the loop must all be on the centreline in the vertical plane, or the bait will spin. Hold the leader and let the bait hang down. Is the hook pulling on the belly? If so, carefully cut a longitudinal slot at the point of entry with a sharp knife so that the hook can move freely. Properly rigged, the bait will be towed by the head loop and won't spin. If it does, tweak the rig until it doesn't or start again.

A small baitfish can also be rigged for trolling with a tandem hooked skirted lure, trade-named a Bait'O Matic by Williamson. Prepare the baitfish as previously described, then pass the front hook through the mouth of the bait so that the bait can move freely from side to side. The front hook should always face upward, and the shank locked into a recess in the lure head. This will ensure that the bait can't rotate in relation to the lure, and the counterweight on the underside of the lurehead will ensure that the whole ensemble doesn't spin. The second hook is pushed through the skin near the tail of the fish.

This ingenious device offers a simple and quick way of rigging natural bait.

Flying fish

Often on passage, a hapless flying fish will land on deck. If you can resist the temptation to pop it under the grill (they're delicious), it will make a great bait. Rig it as described above, but as a finishing touch, extend its wings and hold them in position with soft rigging wire. Poke one end through the leading edge of a wing, secure it with a haywire twist. Run the wire through the head via the eye sockets and attach to the other wing in the same way.

Trolled astern, this bait will behave very much like the real thing – sometimes submerged, at other times skipping along the surface and even taking short flights. You shouldn't have to wait long...

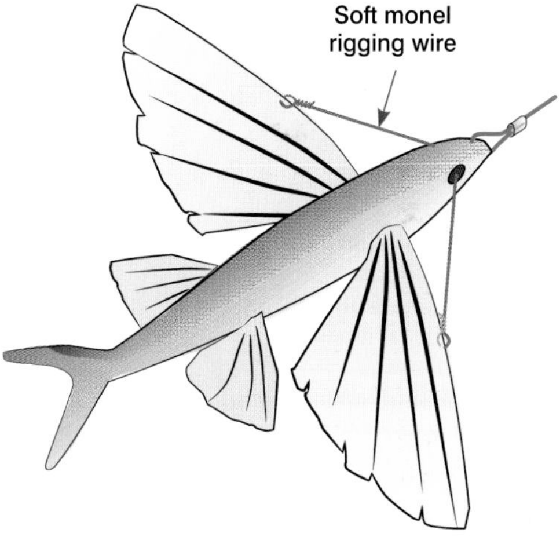

A flying fish rigged as bait – assuming you haven't decided to eat it first, that is.

Ballyhoo

Ballyhoo, a prolific species in tropical waters, are a favourite food of billfish, which slash into the shoals with their bills before engulfing the stunned victims. Netting them for the sport fishing industry is big business – they're the favoured natural bait throughout the Caribbean and many other parts of the world.

As their other name suggests, ballyhoo come equipped with a beak, or the lower half of one to be precise. Because of this, neither the head-loop approach nor the bait-o-matic will work – bespoke rigging methods are required. Sports fishermen often rig them with the hook well forward in the bait. Both these rigs rely on the drop-back technique as described later on page 49, deadly for billfish but not so for toothy varieties that will just chop off the bait abaft the hook. We need to rig them with the hook further aft. This could be done by using a stinger, but I prefer the method shown below.

First, prepare the bait as described previously – remove eyes, eject gut contents, trim off fins and loosen up the backbone. Then break off the beak leaving a stub of about 25mm. If this is done by snapping carefully downwards, a useful groove will be left on the underside of the stub. As we mentioned previously, for a lifelike action, the bait must be towed along by its head. This is achieved by a head-pin in the following rig. The pin is vertical spike of single strand wire, incorporated into the extended haywire twist used to attach the hook in a single-strand wire leader. Here's how:

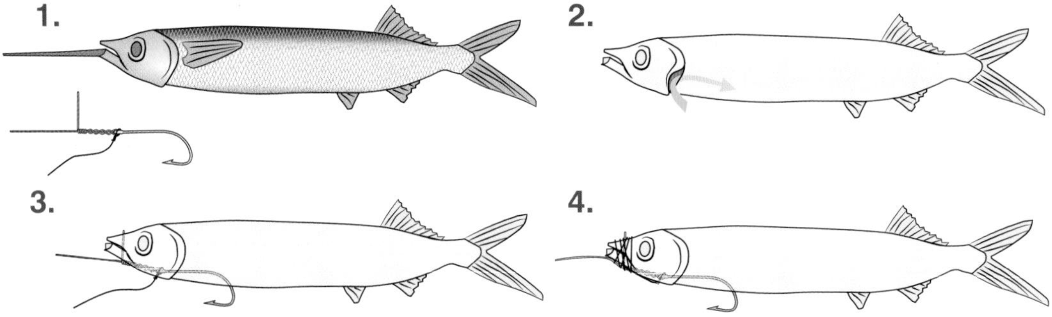

1. **Attach a suitably sized hook with a haywire twist (see Knots section starting page 81). The length of the haywire twist should be such that distance from the final twist to the bend of the hook is just over half the length of the bait. Don't snap off the wire in the normal way, but leave a spike sticking up in the same vertical plane as the hook.**
2. **Insert the hook point under the gill cover and work it through into the body cavity. Bring the hook point out through the belly, leaving the spike under the bait's head. After checking that the hook and the spike are in the same plane, push the spike up and out through the top of the head level with the eyes.**
3. **As before, check that the hook moves freely where it exits the fish's belly.**

4. **You can either lock the spike to the fish's head with a small elastic band by hooking one end of the band over the spike, then wrapping it once or twice around the head before hooking the other end back over the spike. Alternatively, as shown here, you can use monel or light copper wire instead of the elastic band. Poke the wire through the eye sockets, wrap the ends around the head behind the spike and finish off with a few turns around the bill stub, which will locate the leader in the groove we mentioned earlier.**

The completed ballyhoo.

Rigged in this way, your ballyhoo will skip along – or just under the surface. If you want to troll deeper, slide an egg sinker down the line to the head of the bait, and secure it in place with soft wire. The final embellishment is to slide a muppet or small skirted lure down the leader so that it locates against the egg sinker if you're using one, or the nose of the bait if you're not.

But if your target fish is dorado or tuna, you may want to take your chances with wahoo and their toothy chums, and go for a less visible mono leader. 80lb breaking strain is as light as you should go, using one crimp to secure the hook and another to attach the separately formed L-shaped spike in the appropriate position. As an alternative to an egg sinker, a chin weight can be incorporated into the crimped hook connection.

The Stinger Rig

A second hook, often a treble, is attached to the primary hook by a short length of single strand wire. It can be lightly hooked under the skin of the bait, or left loose to stream alongside. Use it when you suspect that fish are short-striking your bait or lure.

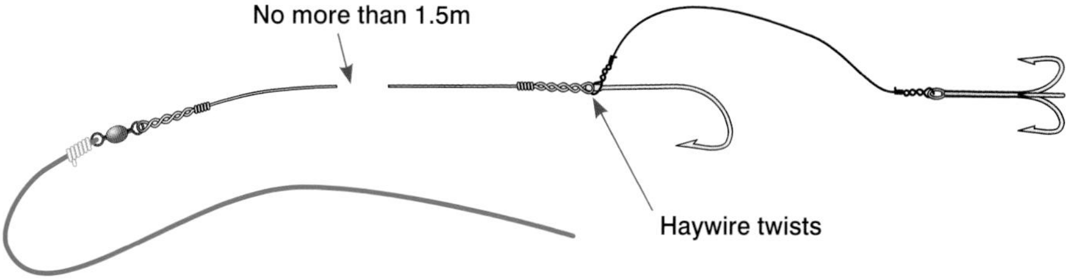

Squid

Again, you must first decide on the leader material. For all but the toothy fellows, heavy mono will be fine. Otherwise my preference would be to use plastic covered multi-strand wire.

1. **Thread the line through a large bead, then through two crimps and finally through the eye of a suitably sized hook, leaving a working end of about 200mm. The bead will drag the squid through the water – there's no load on the hook until a fish grabs it. Don't remove the tentacles, as they'll waggle enticingly just aft of the hook. Rigged in this way, the squid will splash around on the surface. If you want to deploy it below the surface, use a lead egg sinker instead of the bead.**

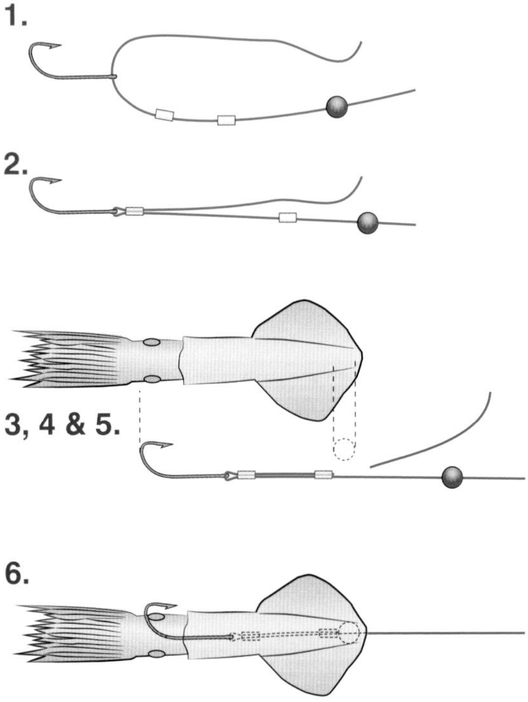

2. **Thread the working end back through both crimps, but not through the bead. Slide the first crimp down to the hook and crimp up. You've now secured the hook, and are left with the 200mm working end. Don't compress the second crimp yet as it needs to be adjusted to suit the size of the squid.**
3. **Lay out the squid with the rig alongside, the bend of the hook level with the squid's eyes and the bead level with the front end of the mantle, then slide up the second crimp to the bead.**
4. **Compress the crimp, then trim off the excess line.**
5. **Cut the standing part of the line to the required leader length. If using mono of 300lb or more, cut it obliquely leaving a sharp point.**
6. **Insert the sharp end of the leader inside the mantle just behind the head, and poke it through at end of the mantle as close to the centre as you can get it. For lighter line use a baiting needle. Pull the line through until the bead fits snugly inside the apex of the mantle and push the hook right through the head between the eyes. Crimp on a swivel in the end of the leader, and you've rigged your squid.**

BOATING YOUR CATCH

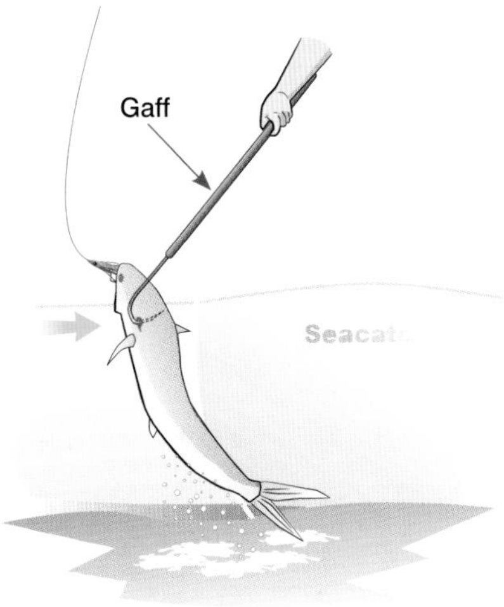

If the gaff has a loop on the handle, do not put your hand through it. Better still, cut the loop off. A big fish could drag you overboard!

Some crews deploy two or more handlines at once, at different depths and with different lures. This will certainly increase the chance of a strike, but not necessarily of a catch. If you get a strike on one line, the other must be brought in very smartly to avoid a foul-up. Ocean predators often hunt in packs, so simultaneous strikes are a real possibility.

Having avoided all these pitfalls, and hauled the fish to the transom, you now face the problem of transferring it from its environment to yours. This needs to be done with some haste, as waving a landing net or a gaff around can induce the fish to take off again at a fair clip. If a net is used, the hooks on the lure are very likely to get caught up in it whilst the fish is still on the wrong side, providing the fish with a welcome last chance of escape. A gaff is much the better implement in my opinion, particularly for larger fish.

Keep the gaff clear of the leader, or a bodged attempt is likely to dislodge the lure from the fish's mouth. Aim to gaff the fish just aft of the head using an overhand action with the hook angled below the shaft. Then lift the fish quickly and smoothly clear of the water and into the boat.

Many fish have sharply spiked fins and razor-like edges to their gills, so handle with care. Barracuda and wahoo in particular have an impressive set of teeth, and a bad attitude. A freshly boated fish, if not fully played out, is also likely to be waving a lure around with a number of spare hooks on it. Attaching yourself to the fish via these is an event likely to remain long in your memory. Tough, rawhide gardening gloves from a previous life are very useful from this point on.

Ending the struggle

Finding itself beached on your cockpit sole, an apparently exhausted fish can get a sudden adrenalin rush. It must be dispatched rapidly. A sharp tap on the head with a winch handle is likely to do nothing other than enrage it further. Some skippers use an icepick to pierce the fish's brain, but it's a very small target even if you know where it is. Full cooperation is also required from the fish by not leaping about. I prefer to pour a little alcohol into its gills, which will kill it more humanely in seconds. In the West Indies, the local 70% proof 'Jack Iron' rum is the stuff for this. Fish die for it. An American pal of mine uses a rum loaded water pistol. He once scared his wife half to death when she caught him taking a surreptitious squirt himself. A third use for this stuff is lighting the barbecue.

Another yachtie told me this, and it seems to work – If you can prevent the fish's tail from touching anything, it's more likely to remain docile on the cockpit sole.

REEL TIME

Many cruisers find a single handline all they need to provide a supply of fresh fish to the galley, but such a rig has its limitations. It must be brutally heavyweight to prevent a large fish from breaking-off once the snubber is fully extended. Consequently the line will be highly visible to the fish and the action of the lure is likely to be inhibited, resulting in fewer strikes. Neither is it without risk to you and your crew. Coils of loose line and a powerful adversary create potential for a serious accident. These limitations can be much reduced by using a suitable reel, securely clamped to the stern rail.

The reel should be of the revolving spool type – either a large centrepin reel such as the Australian-made Alvey, or a multiplier. Fixed spool reels are less suitable for heavy-duty trolling. They are designed primarily for efficient casting, with less importance given to ease of retrieval. This means reeling in can be very hard work.

An Alvey reel – bulky but uncomplicated and dependable. An excellent choice for use on a boat.

Alvey centrepin reels have a narrow, large diameter spool with direct 1:1 gearing. They are used the world over for trolling and bottom fishing. Their smaller models can also be used for casting, by swiveling the reel itself, but the type that will interest boaters the most are straightforward centrepins. Boat fishing versions cover the range from 115mm diameter to an enormous 500mm – the larger sizes intended for commercial fishing. Smaller sizes, up to 230mm diameter can be used with a rod, but above that they're designed to be clamped to a stern rail and used in conjunction with an integral line guide. Models suitable for trolling are equipped with a drag (or clutch) mechanism and an audible ratchet. Their simplicity and robustness makes them a firm favourite with many offshore skippers.

Multipliers are more mechanically complex. They typically have a wide, small diameter spool and gearing up to 5:1 to increase the rate of line recovery. There are a number of different reels on the market but the American-made Penn Senators are difficult to beat – within reason the larger the better. Anything smaller than a size 6/0 won't hold enough line or be man enough to deal with large, powerful fish. A 9/0 would be better still, and a 12/0 even more so. Other high-quality reels include those made by Shimano, Daiwa and Okuma. But whilst these are fine for mackerel and bass, which aren't going to strip off vast quantities of line on their first run, these reels can't match the bigger Senators in terms of the line capacity you'll need for larger fish.

This is a Penn Senator 6/0 – about as small a multiplier as you would want on a boat.

Reel maintenance

All of these reels are very robust and require little maintenance. However the following regime will ensure long-term reliability:

- **After a day's fishing, swill off the reel with fresh water and release the pressure on the drag. A regular spray of moisture repelling lubricant will do no harm at all.**
- **Every few weeks lightly oil or grease the reel's external moving parts, particularly the handles, the ratchet button and the free-spool lever.**
- **At least once a year dismantle the reel and thoroughly clean the various parts, then lubricate with light machine oil or a dab of reel lubricant, and carefully reassemble.**

Living with reels

A hefty Penn Senator 12/0 clamped to a pushpit. Note the 'star' type drag adjustment under the winding handle.

The reel must be securely clamped onto the stern rail or some other convenient point, positioned so the line can't chafe on any part of the boat and to provide plenty of room for the rotation of the handle.

It can be mounted on the back of a vertical stanchion or the top of a horizontal fore-and-aft tube, and should be orientated so that the line comes off the top of the spool and is retrieved when the handle is turned in a clockwise direction. Mounted thus, the handle will be on the right side of the reel. This is ideal for right-handers, but left-handed reels are available from some manufacturers for southpaws. I use a Penn Senator 12/0 loaded with 150lb (68kg) Polyester line and a 10m long 150lb (68kg) breaking strain mono leader, mono being less visible to the fish than polyester and also more resistant to chafing. Once the lure is deployed, the reel is put in gear, the clutch adjusted to give sufficient resistance to set the hook, but not so much as to prevent the fish from taking line, and the ratchet set in the 'on' position.

There's nothing more to do until the glorious screech from the reel announces a striking fish as it streaks off on its first run. Typically, you should expect this to happen while you're in the head, taking a sun sight or other such engaging activity. Adjust the clutch as necessary when reeling in the fish, hardening it when able to recover line and easing it when the fish takes off on another run.

TIP **One of the primary benefits of using a reel is the adjustable drag. This is a clutch mechanism which can be set between 'full on' which allows no slip, and 'full off' which allows line to be drawn off the reel with little resistance. Setting this correctly will limit the tension that the fish can induce in the line, absorbing the initial shock loads and practically eliminating break-offs. Lighter, and hence less visible line can be used as you're no longer dependent on the ultimate strength of your rig to resist the power of a hooked fish.**

When winding in the line a thumb can be used to control distribution over the spool. Just visible is a wahoo, about to be brought on board.

Even non-fisher crew members instinctively leap into action when the reel sings out. But false alarms can occur. I was at the chart table, the cockpit temporarily vacated. Suddenly, a partially-clad female crewmember leaped from her bunk and bounded gazelle-like into the cockpit past a bemused, but grateful, skipper. Only when Mary, hearing all the commotion, emerged from the heads clutching an electric toothbrush, did I understand the reason for this strange behaviour. Sadly, my subsequent trials with the toothbrush have so far failed to achieve a repeat performance.

Maintaining contact with a running fish by reel is easier than with a handline, and its chance of throwing the hook is significantly reduced.

As line is recovered it must be spread back and forth across the full width of the spool using the thumb of the non-winding hand. If this isn't done, coils of line will build up locally before collapsing and becoming trapped under successive coils, which will cause a break-off should the fish decide to take line again. You'll find it easier to spread the line if the reel is mounted on a horizontal tube, rather than on the back of a vertical stanchion where your access to the line will be impeded.

'Alacazam' was about 300 miles north west of the Cape Verdes, on passage for the West Indies. My 'favourite' lure of the moment, a Rapella Sliver which imitates an immature garfish, had been unproductive for a while. Suspecting fouled hooks I was reeling it back to the boat to clear it when I noticed something shadowing it. The fish, a large bull dorado, followed the lure right to the transom. I stopped winding to avoid pulling the lure out of the water. The dorado stopped too, just a couple feet aft of the lure, studying it intently. Suddenly it struck and ran, and in my haste to adjust the clutch I knocked the reel into free spool. By this time the fish was in top gear and heading for the horizon, unsportingly refusing to even slow down.

Still struggling with the clutch, the free spool lever and the ratchet, I could easily have lost a finger in the coils of line that were spooling off the reel. An enormous overrun developed, a loud crack was heard and that was the last I saw of my favourite lure. Another lesson learned, fortunately without injury. Always take great care when playing powerful fish.

TIP **A fish may well strike when you're reeling the lure back to the boat. Be prepared for this by having the clutch set only just tight enough to recover line without slipping.**

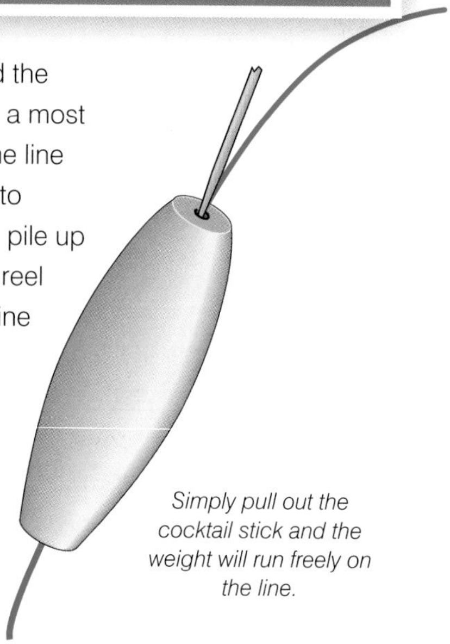

Simply pull out the cocktail stick and the weight will run freely on the line.

You'll find that a large fish won't want to stay directly behind the boat when hooked – it'll swim off to one side or the other in a most uncooperative manner. If you maintain a constant course the line will come off the reel obliquely, and you'll find it impossible to spread it evenly across the spool. If you keep winding it will pile up against one side of the spool and eventually jam under the reel structure. Your only option is to drop the sails, start the engine and manoeuvre the boat to keep the fish astern. Single-handers will experience something of a dilemma here – more so if the fish dives under the boat.

Another problem will arise if you're using a fixed trolling weight. Whilst the swivel connection between your main line and the leader can be wound onto the reel, the weight, of course, can't and will prevent you from winding in your catch right up to the transom. To get around this problem you can use a barrel lead rather than the trolling weight. These are drilled longitudinally, and are normally prevented from sliding down to the lure by an appropriately positioned swivel. But forget the swivel – secure the weight in place by piece of a cocktail stick, or a sharpened matchstick jammed in the hole at one end of the weight. Then, when it arrives at the reel during retrieve, pull out the stick allowing the weight to slide down to the lure. Even so, you still need to handle the leader when the fish is close to the transom, to position it for gaffing.

HOW ALLURING THE LURE?

A word on 'favourite' lures. It works like this. You catch a good fish on a particular lure. In the knowledge that it duped at least one fish you continue to use it, disregarding all others. It catches more fish from time to time and so becomes your favourite. You continue to use it through long blank spells believing that 'if this doesn't work, nothing will'. Wrong! The status of favourite has been established on the basis of time in the water rather than catch rate. If you're not catching, try something different. You could end up with a whole box of ex-favourites. It's a bit like serial monogamy.

But before you randomly select a different lure, think through the possible reasons why you're not catching. Could it be that:

- **The lure has picked up some weed or other flotsam or jetsam?**
- **You're sailing too quickly or slowly for the lure to operate as it was designed to?**
- **The lure is too large or too small to interest the fish or too close to the surface and the fish are feeding some distance below – which may well be the case on bright days with the sun high in the sky – or vice versa?**
- **You're simply using the wrong lure? Perhaps the fish are feeding on sandeels and you're trying to tempt them with an imitation squid.**

So ask yourself these questions and select the next lure accordingly. Of course it could be that there are no fish in your patch of sea, or those that are just aren't feeding, in which case your choice of lure will be entirely academic.

So whilst a reel solves most of the problems associated with a handline, it doesn't solve them all and creates a few new ones of its own. Which is why you should consider using a rod.

Rods bring advantages

The immediate benefits of using a rod are:

- **The line is always delivered to the centre of the reel spool via the line guides on the rod, ready for you to spread it evenly with your thumb**
- **The natural movement of the rod tip caused by the pitching and rolling of the boat and the wave action on the line imparts a darting action to the lure, further increasing its appeal**
- **On removing the rod from its holder you can properly drive the hooks home, and now you're in direct contact you can have much greater control over your fish**
- **The flexibility of the rod absorbs some of the fish's power when it changes speed or direction**
- **You can now move around the cockpit, reducing the need for sudden and radical course changes**
- **You will now experience the thrill of playing a fish. You're fully involved – it's personal!**

Then there's safety...

For me though, the most compelling reason for using a rod is one of safety. A rod enables the fish to be brought to the gaff without any need to handle the leader.

But if, like 'Alacazam', your yacht sports a stern gantry laden with solar panels, a radar scanner, a wind generator and various lights and antenna, you'll now become aware of a downside to this otherwise useful structure. You're left with an access window half the width of the transom through which to play the fish, bounded on one side by the gantry and the other by the backstay. We've had many a hairy moment passing the rod around the structure – no sooner than you've completed the transfer the fish decides he'd rather be back where he was. Davits or a windvane self-steering gear can make it even more awkward, but then everything's a trade-off on a sailboat. In this regard, motor boats with their spacious cockpits and broad, uncluttered sterns are much more convenient.

There are often dozens of surrounding impediments when fishing off a sailing boat.

BIG IS NOT BEST

Many boat rods are around 2m long, but shorter rods of around 1.65m, known as 'stand-up' rods, are best for trolling from sailboats. They're convenient to stow and are sufficiently powerful to subdue a hard-fighting game fish. The longer the rod, the more strain will be applied to your arms and shoulders. The fish has the advantage of extra leverage.

Rods are classified in terms of the power they can exert on a hooked fish. This power is measured by the test curve of the rod. A rod of 50lb test curve (ie a 50lb class rod) requires a force of 50lb applied at its tip to bend it through 90° and would normally be used with 50lb breaking strain line. There are six main classes recognized by the International Game Fishing Association (IGFA) – 12lb, 20lb, 30lb, 50lb, 80lb and 130lb.

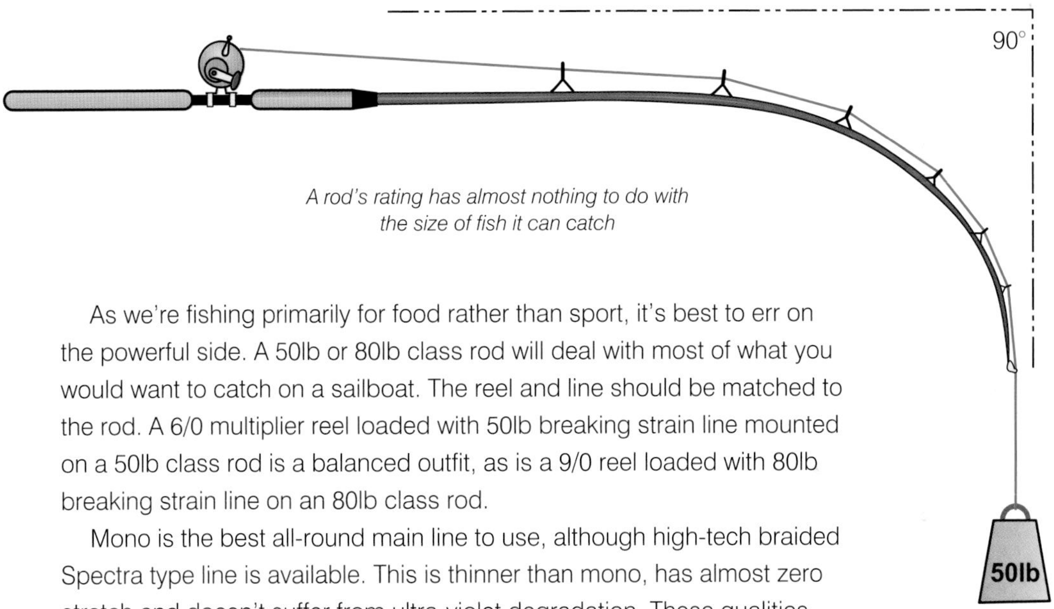

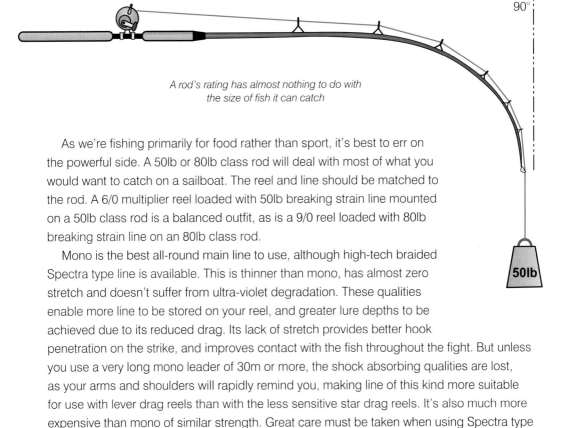

A rod's rating has almost nothing to do with the size of fish it can catch

As we're fishing primarily for food rather than sport, it's best to err on the powerful side. A 50lb or 80lb class rod will deal with most of what you would want to catch on a sailboat. The reel and line should be matched to the rod. A 6/0 multiplier reel loaded with 50lb breaking strain line mounted on a 50lb class rod is a balanced outfit, as is a 9/0 reel loaded with 80lb breaking strain line on an 80lb class rod.

Mono is the best all-round main line to use, although high-tech braided Spectra type line is available. This is thinner than mono, has almost zero stretch and doesn't suffer from ultra-violet degradation. These qualities enable more line to be stored on your reel, and greater lure depths to be achieved due to its reduced drag. Its lack of stretch provides better hook penetration on the strike, and improves contact with the fish throughout the fight. But unless you use a very long mono leader of 30m or more, the shock absorbing qualities are lost, as your arms and shoulders will rapidly remind you, making line of this kind more suitable for use with lever drag reels than with the less sensitive star drag reels. It's also much more expensive than mono of similar strength. Great care must be taken when using Spectra type line, as its low stretch, high strength and small diameter give it garrotte-like qualities under tension.

The rod tip line-guide at least should be of the roller type, and there's much to be said for having roller guides throughout. These reduce friction and wear and tear on the line.

A rod of this type is designed to be used 'upside down' with the line guides uppermost, in conjunction with a multiplier reel. A properly designed rod will have the line guides spaced such that even under high load the line will remain clear of the rod.

Alternatively you could use a plain ringed rod with a centrepin reel mounted below, where the issue of the line touching the rod doesn't arise. The rings at the very least must have aluminium oxide or carbide inserts or they'll corrode and destroy your line.

A mono shock leader of around double the strength of the main line should be used, to be capable of withstanding abrasion from the flanks of the fish or parts of the boat. It should be inspected regularly for damage and replaced as necessary. Make sure it's long enough to have several turns on the reel when the fish is within about 10m of the transom.

Don't use a link-swivel at this join as it'll jam in the rod tip roller, leaving your fish smugly cruising about astern, safely beyond the reach of the gaff. When this happens you have no option other than to haul in the fish by hand, which I regard as a safety issue and is best avoided. Instead, tie the leader to the loop in the main line with a uni-knot. If the resulting knot is still too big to pass through the end roller, you'll need to use a smaller diameter leader.

A 50lb main line and a 100lb leader works fine for my outfit. You'll need at least one swivel in your rig to avoid twists developing in your line, but providing this is no more than 2m to 3m from your lure, you should still be able to gaff your fish without handling the leader.

To avoid any risk of the fish chomping through your shock leader, you can attach your lure via a short wire trace.

Renowned for its delicate flesh, this wahoo would feed several crews!

Drop-back technique

One very cunning trick I learned from a big-game charter skipper in Trinidad is the use of the drop-back technique. Sometimes a fish, particularly a billfish, will strike a baitfish to kill or stun it before engulfing it completely. If your lure, despite having been dealt with in this fashion nonchalantly swims on, the predator is likely to be unimpressed and will decline your invitation.

The drop-back trick lets the lure stop for a second or two as would a stunned fish, whereupon the predator grabs it. To achieve this desirable outcome bring the line from the rod tip back to a quick-release clip attached to the gantry or other point on the boat. The resulting slack in the line when snatched from the quick-release clip for the short time before the boat catches up lets the lure stop in the water. You can buy purpose-made clips, or make one from a plastic clothes peg and rubber band.

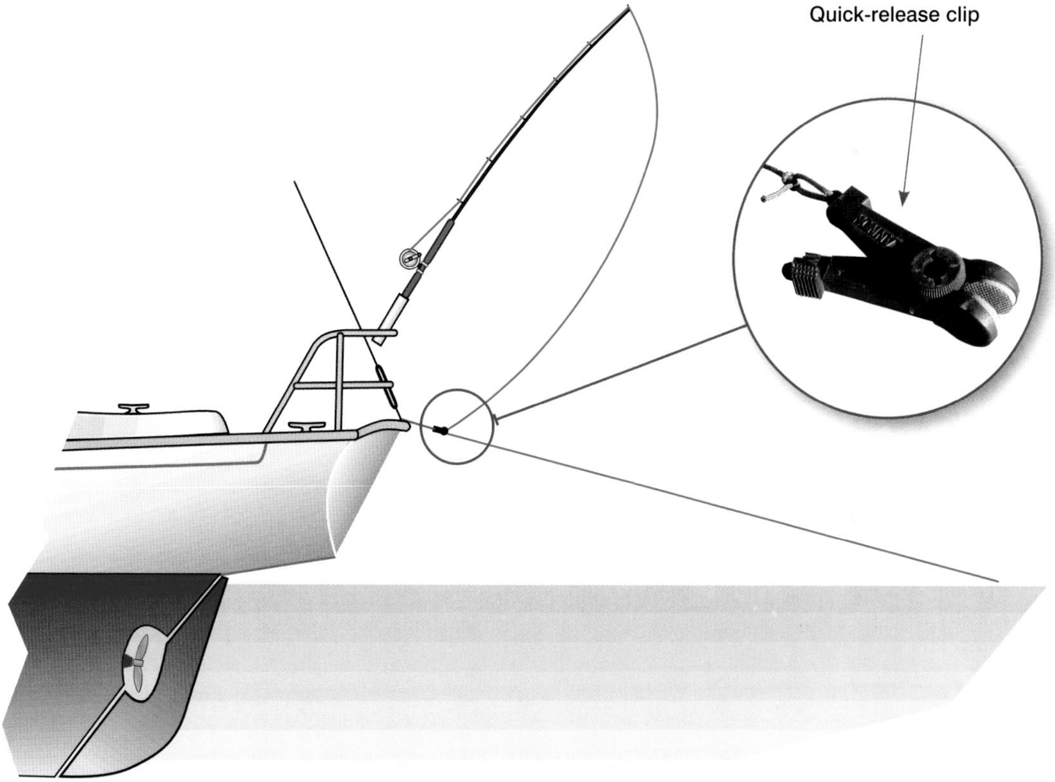

Fool the fish into thinking it's got its prey. It will come as something of a surprise for it when the line comes tight.

A Multi-lure Spread

Your chances of a hook-up are clearly increased if you have a selection of lures deployed. The benefits include:

- **More lures will create more noise in the water, and hence be more stimulating to the fish**
- **You can offer the fish different types and sizes of lures**
- **You can cover various depths**
- **You can deploy your lures at different distances from your transom**

A typical offshore sportfishing boat will often use up to seven rods, with long outriggers hauled out each side to spread the lures over a 15m wide swathe of the ocean. The lines are attached to the outriggers by quick release clips, which release the line when a fish hits the lure. Some lures will be set short – that is, close to the boat – whilst others set long, with each lure's position carefully adjusted to put it in the face of one of the series of following waves generated by the boat itself (see page 31). If there's one on the centreline – the 'shotgun' – it should be the furthest aft, intended to entice any curious onlookers at all the activity ahead. A general rule is that the larger, most active lures should be closer to the boat – conventional wisdom dictating that a fish is disinclined to swim past a large offering to get to a small one.

Now I'm not suggesting that skippers should festoon their boats with rods in this fashion, but one from each corner of the transom is a reasonable proposition for a monohull. This is what we have on 'Alacazam', with a teaser spreader bar set on the centreline. If conditions are right, we use the taffrail mounted reel as well, with a bird teaser and a daisy chain set short.

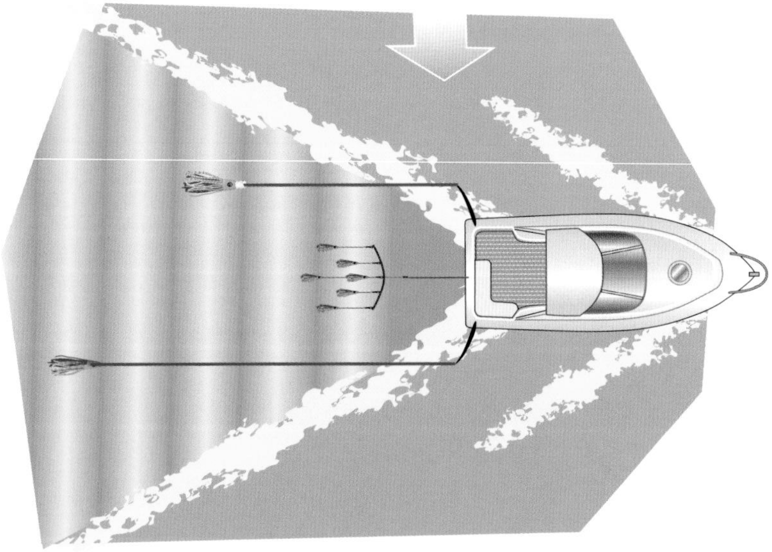

Increase your chances by deploying more lines. Powerboats can trail several. And don't forget to rig fish-attracting teasers – often more productive than an extra lure.

If you do opt for using more than one lure, you need to take the wind direction into consideration. The higher the rod tip is, the greater length of line there is exposed to the force of the wind. With the wind on the beam, the lines get blown down to leeward, so to keep them apart the windward lure should be closer to the boat. If you don't want to increase the distance behind the boat of the leeward lure, you can bring the windward one forward by passing the line through a quick release clip attached to a low point on the transom. This will reduce the length of line clear of the sea and allow you to position your lure closer to the boat. If you need to tack or gybe, you'll have to adjust your lines accordingly.

Getting Down Deeper

Most of the time you'll pick up tuna and dorado on or close to the surface, but if you're after wahoo, kingfish or other large mackerel types your catch rate should improve if you can get your lure 10m or more below the surface. These depths can be achieved by deep-diving swimming plugs, or by using a planer, or a combination of the two.

Planers of any size can be used with handlines since, like paravanes, they trip when a fish is hooked. The heavier stainless steel ones tend to dive deeper and be more powerful than their plastic cousins. A planer will normally set in the dive position upon entering the water, but if it doesn't, or trips unaccountably, it can be reset without having to bring it back in again. Just snatch in a couple of metres then quickly release it. The resultant slack in the line should allow the planer to nosedive and reset itself. Use the same technique to trip it for retrieval, or – particularly with a large one – be prepared for an arms and shoulders work-out.

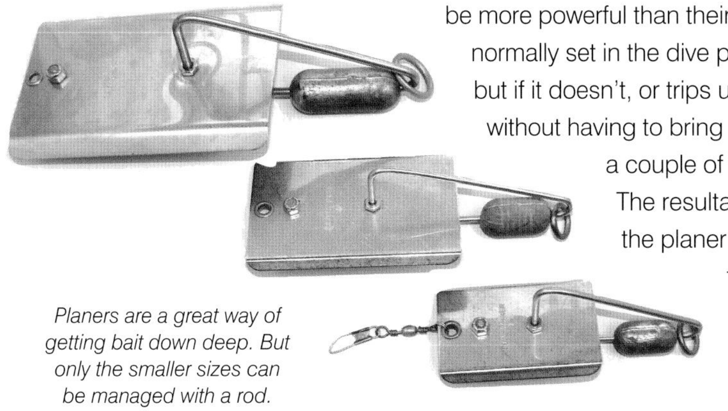

Planers are a great way of getting bait down deep. But only the smaller sizes can be managed with a rod.

Downrigger

The smaller planers can be used with your trolling rod, but larger ones will create too much drag. And as mentioned earlier you'll need a leader of at least 7m, which means you'll have to resort to hauling your fish in by hand when the planer arrives at the rod tip – and you already know my views on that.

But this inconvenience is avoided by using your planer as part of a downrigger set-up. Not the full-on big-game sports boat version involving a crane-like structure on the afterdeck and a heavy lead ball, but a simple adaptation of it perfectly suited for sailboats and motorboats. The essence of a downrigger is that the planer is deployed on its own line, and is only temporarily connected to the trolling line by a quick-release clip. When a fish takes the lure, the release clip does its thing, leaving the now redundant planer to be retrieved independently.

Here's how to deploy your downrigger:

- **First, let out your trolling line until the lure is 10m or so behind the boat, then**
- **Attach the line to the release clip on the downrigger, then**
- **With the reel in gear, but with the clutch adjusted such that it will give line without overrunning, slowly ease out the planer line to its full extent, then**
- **Adjust the clutch to the appropriate setting, set the ratchet and await further development.**

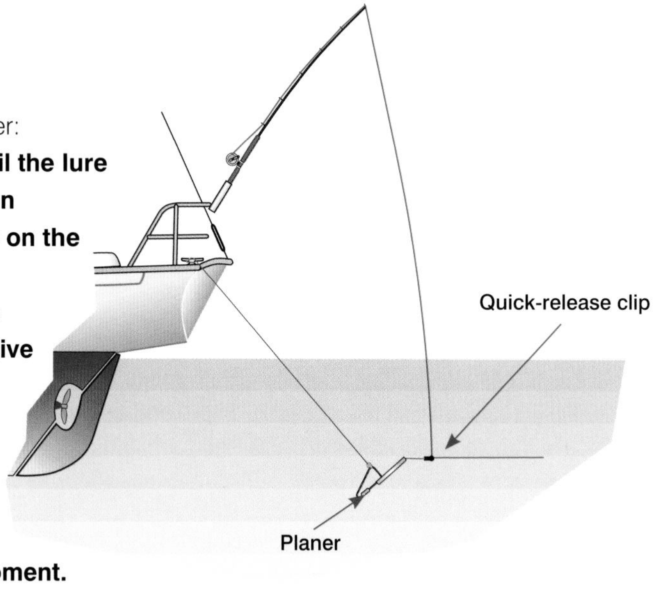

The apparent disadvantage of a downrigger is that each time you deploy your trolling gear you have to haul in the planer to reconnect the mainline to the quick release clip. But there's a way around this. All you need is a good supply of elastic bands and a few link swivels:

- **Set the downrigger to the required depth, without attaching your mainline or even the quick release clip (which you no longer need).**
- **Commence deployment of your line from your trolling rod, but stopping the line when the lure is about 12m or so behind the boat.**
- **Attach an elastic band to the swivel (not the link) of the link swivel by putting one end through the other and pulling it tight, then**
- **Attach the elastic band to the trolling line in a similar fashion, then connect the trolling line to the planer towline using the link of the link swivel.**
- **Release the mainline slowly allowing the link swivel to be drawn along the downwardly angled towing line by the drag of the lure, until it's stopped by a bead fixed a short distance above the planer.**

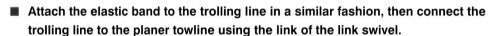

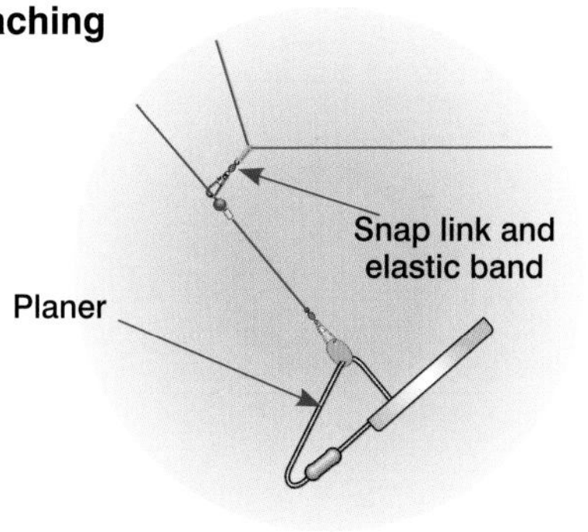

When a fish takes, the elastic band will break, leaving the mainline free of the towline and the planer in place ready for you to do it all over again with a new link swivel and elastic band. When you eventually bring in the downrigger, you'll be able to recover the link swivels for future use.

Without the drag of the lure, the planer – providing it hasn't tripped – will now dive deeper and swing forward. Even so there's every chance that a hooked fish will wrap the towing line and the trolling line together, so – be warned!

Planer Limitations

The depth to which a planer dives depends on the area of the plate, the speed of the tow and the length of mainline. As a general rule of thumb, expect around 5m of depth for each 10m of line deployed. Theoretically, for any given size of planer and constant towing speed, the more line out the deeper the planer will dive. So if 20m of line out gets you down 10m then it doesn't seem unreasonable to suppose that 40m will get you twice that depth. Sadly, the law of diminishing returns says that it won't. The more line out, the greater becomes the line drag, which lowers the planer's angle of attack and eventually trips it. The optimum distance/depth relationship ultimately depends on the diameter and density of the line, and can only be properly assessed by trial and error.

Wire line

Wire gets to greater depths than mono or polyester because its greater density makes it sink more rapidly, while its smaller diameter (for any given strength) creates less drag.

Trolling wire is produced in one of two materials – single-strand stainless steel or single-strand monel wire. Stainless steel wire is not particularly malleable, breaking easily when kinked and making it quite difficult to tie a haywire twist in. Monel, a nickel-copper alloy, is more pliable and kink resistant. It's also denser and consequently sinks more rapidly and stays deeper than stainless. Although more expensive, its better performance and reliability makes monel the favoured material of most wire line trollers. Both stainless and monel are available in several breaking strains of between 15lb and 80lb (6.8kg and 36.2kg) and are normally sold in 100m spools, two of which may be connected.

As a general rule, when trolling at 3 to 4 knots, each 20m of monel line deployed will get your lure down about 2m, so 100m will achieve a trolling depth of around 10m. Trolling with a greater length of wire line than this tends to be counterproductive, as the cumulative drag causes the line to plane back up. Used in conjunction with a deep-diving plug, trolling depths of up to 15m can be achieved without the use of an inline sinker.

A rail mounted centrepin reel like an Alvey (see page 40) is a convenient way to fish with a wire line, but if you choose to use a rod, then the outfit needs to be specialized to a degree.

First, the reel shouldn't have an aluminium spool as the resulting galvanic action will destroy the spool. A Penn Senator 6/0 which has a cast chrome-over-bronze spool would be a good choice, loaded with 100m of 50lb monel and 300m of mono or Polyester backing. When trolling make sure that all the wire is in the water, as this will give you the greatest depth and avoid undue wear to the guides on the rod.

Next, the rod can't have standard issue guides, as the wire will cut grooves in them in no time at all. Ring guides must be tungsten carbide, but my preference is to use a rod with roller guides throughout, accepting the higher degree of maintenance that comes with a rod of this kind. Wire line of any kind must be used with great care, as a trip to the cheese counter at your local supermarket will demonstrate. I recommend the use of a long mono leader so that when your catch is close to the boat all the wire is safely back on the reel.

BIG GAME LEVER DRAG REELS

A reel of the star-drag type will do the job, but for ultimate control you may consider a single-speed or even a two-speed lever drag type reel such as a Penn International to be worth the expense. Designed for dealing with the world's toughest gamefish, they're very well engineered and will last a lifetime. Predictably perhaps, they're very expensive. But the lever drag is much more controllable than a star-drag, and can be preset to operate between free-spool and a setting just below the point at which the line will break – the strike drag setting. Remember that as with all multiplier reels, the more line a fish takes, the more rapidly the diameter of the remaining line on the spool reduces. As the effect of the drag is proportional to the diameter of the spooled line, you should adjust the drag setting accordingly.

If you have a spring balance aboard you can use this to set the strike drag.

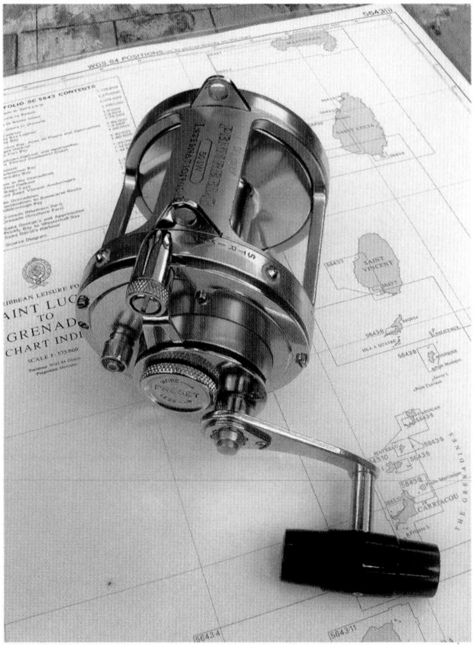

Instead of the star type drag adjustment, this top quality Penn International reel uses a lever which can be seen above the winding handle.

TIP Always rig a lanyard securing the rod to the boat, just in case.

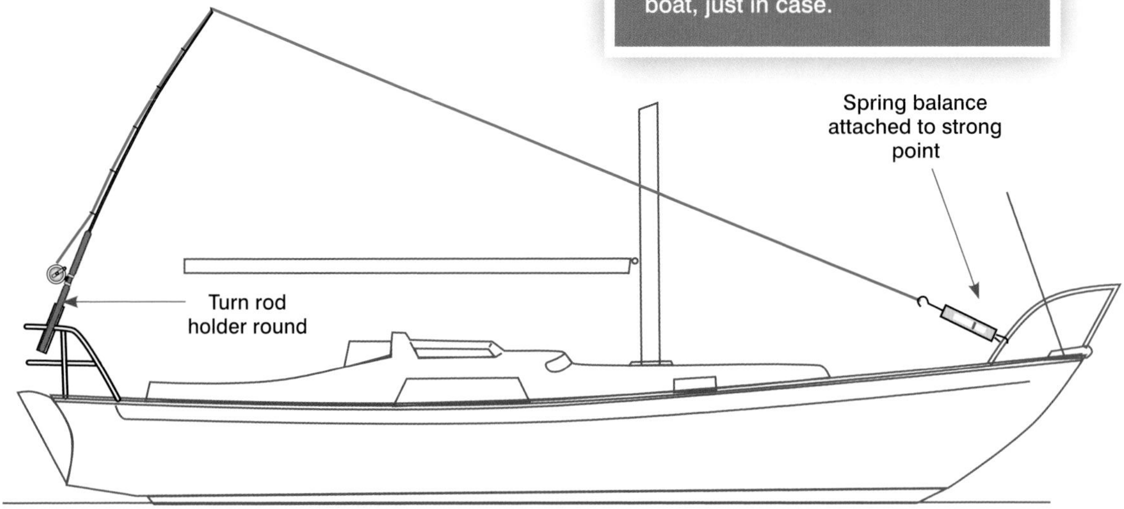

Lever drag reels can be preset to ease the line at a point well before the line or its attachments will break. As you wind on the tension, a spring balance will show the load.

With the rod placed securely in the holder and the spring balance positioned so that the line is around 90° to the rod, adjust the drag setting so that the scale reads between 25% and 33% of the main line breaking strain when the drag starts to slip. 50lb test line should have a strike drag setting of between 12½lb and 17lb (5.7kg and 8kg). This will allow for the weak points which unavoidably occur at knotted and crimped connections.

The rod should be located in a rod holder firmly fixed to the structure of the boat, either clamped to the pushpit or recessed into the cockpit coamings. The holder can be made from a short length of thick-walled rigid plastic pipe of an appropriate diameter lashed to the pushpit, providing that you can find some way of orientating it about 30° from the vertical. Or you can splash out on a stainless steel, fully adjustable version.

You can leave your lures ready rigged if you make yourself a DIY storage tube – here seen lashed to the rod holder. The lure hooks onto the loop of mono before it's wound upwards into the tube out of harm's way.

There'll be times when the rod isn't in use, but still in the holder on the sternrail. Maybe you've caught all you need, or the conditions aren't suitable for fishing. It's tempting just to hook the lure on the reel. Don't. Either detach it, or stow it in a plastic tube lashed to the rodholder or a stanchion where it can't cause harm to boat or crew.

PLAYING THE FISH

Suddenly the reel screams and the rod takes on a satisfying curve – a fish is on!

Things get complicated at this point if you're the only crewmember on watch. On 'Alacazam', normally a two-handed boat, the cry of "Fish On!" gets the off-watch crew up in a hurry. After setting the hook and adjusting the clutch, the rod is returned to the rod holder leaving the fish to fend for itself while we slow the boat down. I then retrieve any other lures we may have out, and Mary hauls in the downrigger and the teaser if either is deployed. Then she disconnects the self-steering and hand steers if necessary.

Only then is any complaining of the "but I was asleep" variety allowed. It's all too easy from this point on to have all pairs of eyes looking astern. Do remember to keep a lookout at all times, and take care in the cockpit. Inadvertent course changes can be readily achieved by knocking off the electronic tiller pilot with a wayward foot, or by allowing the line to hold over the wind vane on the self-steering gear. An accidental gybe is best avoided.

Playing a large fish can be an arduous business. The trick is not to hurry the contest.

If the fish is large and obstinate it may be necessary to drop the sails and manoeuvre under power. Don't be in a rush to get the fish to the transom. It'll be much easier to boat if it's exhausted, and the cockpit of a sailing boat is no place for a powerful, energetic fish with malicious intent.

The fish should be allowed to run against the drag set to provide enough resistance to tire it, but well within the capacity of the rig. If you're using a lever drag reel, then this will be the preset strike drag, but with a star drag it will be the 'that's about right' setting. Between runs 'pump' the rod to recover line. This is done by repeatedly raising the rod to the vertical or just beyond, then lowering it to around 30° while simultaneously cranking in on the reel.

It's vital that pressure is kept on the fish at all times. Any slack in the line and the fish is likely to throw the hook. All this can be a lot harder work than I normally like to become involved in. But keep the pressure on – remember if you rest so does the fish and his recovery rate is probably better than yours.

You'll find playing a large fish much easier if you use a gimballed butt pad. This is not the cosmetic enhancement to which an internet search may lead you. The product I'm referring to comprises a socket for your rod butt and a strap to locate it in front of you, where the action is.

Most stand-up rods have a slot in the steel butt fitting which locates over the bar in the butt pad. A full harness, which hooks onto lugs on top of the reel, will enable you to apply more power against the fish and take some of the load off your arms and shoulders. But now you're directly connected to the fish, so a large one and a jammed reel could pull you straight out of the cockpit. More than one big-game fisherman has been lost in this way, so I should stick to just the butt pad if I were you. After all, in extremis you can always let go of the rod.

The flexibility of the rod, the elasticity of the main line together with the catenary it takes up due to its drag through the water all conspire in absorbing the fish's energy. Coupled with your judicious use of the reel's drag setting, few fish will be capable of applying enough tension in the line to break it – providing you have enough of it left on the reel.

The loads at the butt of the rod can be fearsome. A cupped pad provides useful protection.

But the odds will swing into the fish's favour when you have it within a few yards of the transom. Now there's no catenary in the line, any capacity for line stretch is minimal, the rod is likely to be bent to the limit of its power curve and the line is sawing away merrily against the self-steering gear. A sudden desperate lunge of the fish now may well snap your main line – which is why you should use a shock leader, long enough to have a few turns already on your reel. At the first opportunity try and see how well the fish is hooked. If the fish is only lightly hooked there's a risk that the lure will be torn from its mouth, whereupon it may fly straight into the cockpit and cause injury to you or the crew. Be ready to duck and turn away, and warn other crew members not involved in the boating of the fish to keep well clear. It's also worth wearing sunglasses, which will give you some level of protection against a flying lure.

CHAPTER 3

Adrift and at Anchor

Could you ask for more? A delightful anchorage, a cool drink within reach, and fish for the pan just waiting to be caught. Bliss!

Trolling is probably the most synergetic fishing technique for a sailing boat. The boat's motion through the water provides animation to the lure and, once you're sure that you've got the correct rig deployed and it's at the right depth, you can forget about it. Life aboard continues normally until a fish hits the lure, when things liven up considerably. But if your boat speed falls below a couple of knots, the action of your trolled lure, particularly if it's of the skirted type, will become much less convincing. You may wish to resort to the iron topsail at this point to maintain your passage plan but if you're content to dawdle a while, bring in the trolling gear and try a spot of jigging – a process that simply involves lowering specialised lures into the water and 'jigging' them up and down.

Jigging

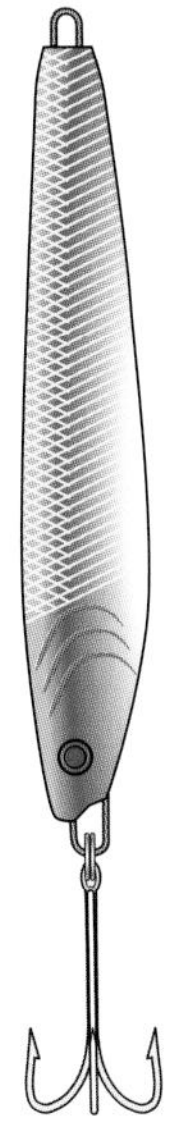

A typical pirk. Heavy and streamlined to get it down to the bottom quickly.

Broken ground, reefs and wrecks often hold a resident fish population and are great for a spot of jigging. Those of you with an electronic fish-finder unit are at an advantage here. Not only will you get a better indication of the true nature of the seabed, but also of congregations of fish. Some of the latest units are capable of distinguishing between shoals of smaller fish and larger individual specimens. In UK and other northern European waters, members of the cod and haddock family may be grubbing around amongst the rocks for food. The traditional deep-water jigging lure for these demersal species is a pirk. Often lead filled, these heavy lures are chrome plated or brightly coloured, normally sport a single treble hook, and designed to sink quickly. They can be fished alone, or used at the end of a multi-lured rig.

My preference is to use a Dexter Wedge (see page 17) as the pirk, in conjunction with a couple of muppets on short snoods above the pirk. Muppets are one-piece moulded lures designed to imitate squid. Many anglers rig them incorrectly by pushing the hook point through the nose of the muppet and threading them over the hook until the eye is concealed inside the nose. This looks fine until it's been in the water for a while, after which the drag of the water will have pulled the muppet over the hook eye leaving it attached on the bend of the hook.

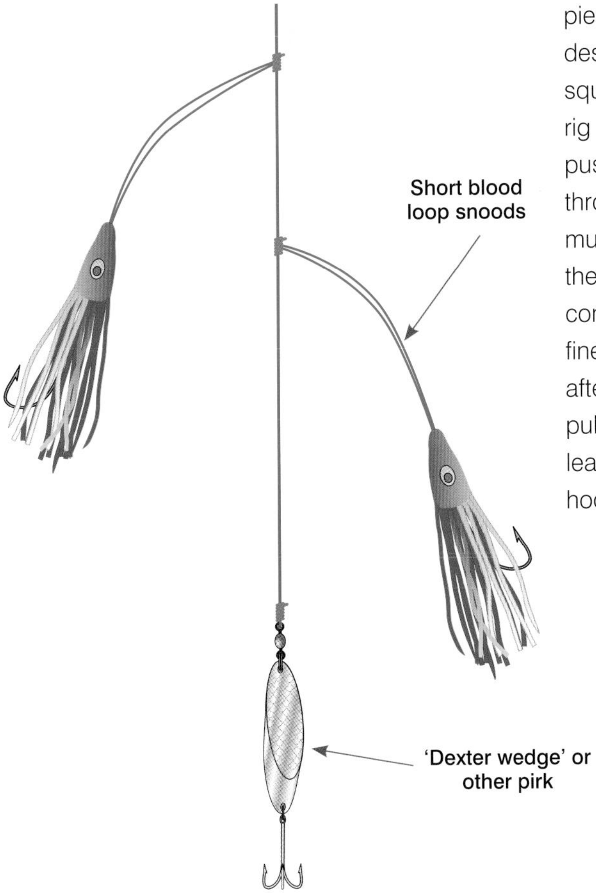

When a fish grabs it, short of the hook point, it's goodbye muppet and no fish. The correct way is to put a hole through the nose with a sewing needle, or better still a hot wire which will seal the edge of the hole. Then push the line through the hole, thread on a small bead and tie on the hook. The bead will then sit nicely inside the head of the muppet leaving the hook-point about two-thirds of the way back, where it should be.

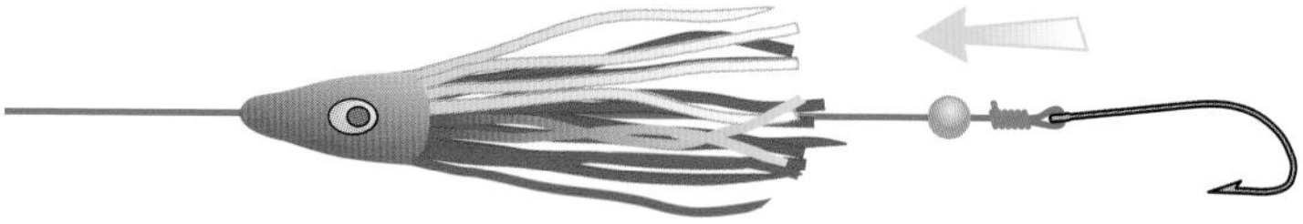

When rigging a muppet don't forget the bead. The hook could pull through if you do.

For jigging, my first choice is to use a rod and reel as you're able to apply much more action to the lure than with a handline. When jigging close to the seabed, the technique is to lower the pirk until you feel it touch bottom, then quickly take a couple of turns on the reel to avoid snagging. Sweep the rod upwards, then lower it allowing the lures to flutter back down again. Repeat the process until you hook a fish or your arms drop off. But if it is a wreck you're over, then you can expect to get caught up now and again whatever you do.

An alternative approach to 'pirking' is to use a soft plastic lure and a flying-collar rig, as shown below. The flying-collar arrangement is said to prevent any tangles on the way down, but I find you can normally get away with a three-way swivel instead, providing you control the rate of descent. With a weight rather than a pirk at the lowest point there is much less chance of snagging on the seabed or the wreck. The technique is different too. Lower the weight until you feel it touch, then reel up slowly about twenty turns or so, and repeat as before. When you get a take, don't strike, just carry on winding. The fish, if it had just grabbed the tail of the lure will take another gulp – and you've got him!

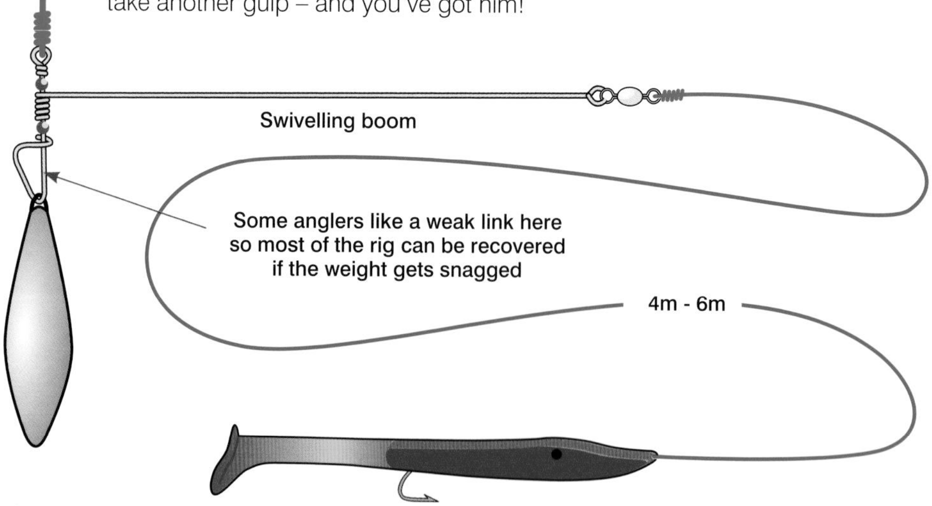
Swivelling boom
Some anglers like a weak link here so most of the rig can be recovered if the weight gets snagged
4m - 6m

Broken ground and reefs in shallower waters are favourite haunts of bass, but the deep-water rig described above can be a little too brutal for this application. A soft plastic bodied lure used on its own is likely to be more effective.

Bucktail jigs come in a variety of shapes, sizes and colours. It pays to carry a selection.

Until the arrival of soft plastic lures, bucktail jigs were the favoured approach, particularly in the United States. These were traditionally made with hair from the tail of a buck (male deer) and still have many devotees. Exotic versions were once made with polar bear hair but these days synthetic materials are used – presumably much to the appreciation of polar bears everywhere.

Bare moulded lead-heads for bucktail jigs are readily available and can be easily made up aboard – just the thing if a dead deer turns up on the foredeck.

Bream

A fish we haven't mentioned yet, the black bream, also frequents this type of seabed. This member of the porgy family isn't an abundant species around our shores, but there are known hotspots. Many summers ago I fished for these on a charter boat out of Littlehampton in Sussex. The skipper would anchor his boat just uptide of the Kingsmere Rocks and we'd enjoy great sport on light tackle using long flowing traces baited with small strips of fresh mackerel. If one attacks your bait, you'll feel it rattle your rod top two or three times. You'll need to strike very quickly as they seldom hook themselves. If you fail to make contact your hook is probably too large. Scale down to a size 4 fine-wire Mustad Aberdeen hook and try again. They won't be a regular catch, but you'll find them quite delicious when they do put in an appearance. Using this technique over rough ground in the Mediterranean you can add other species of sea bream, such as giltheads, to your likely catch. Giltheads are prolific throughout the Mediterranean, and are often caught underway when trolling a small lure. At anchor mullet tactics work well. They can be caught at dusk or dawn simply by allowing a small bread-baited hook to float on the surface near your boat. Incidentally, the local name for giltheads is 'dorade' (French) or 'dorada' (Spanish) neither of which should be confused with the dorado (or mahé mahé).

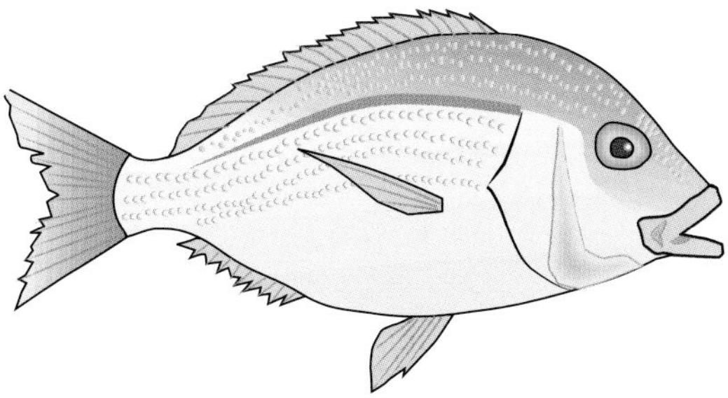

Gilthead breams have a wonderful flavour and are an ideal size to be cooked whole on a barbecue.

In the tropical waters of the Caribbean you could reasonably expect croakers, drums, groupers, grunts, porgies and snappers. Your cook isn't going to turn his nose up at any of these.

If the seabed below you is featureless sand or mud, or you're too far off soundings for it to matter what it is, pelagic species will again become your quarry. Without any clue as to where the fish might be, you'll need to experiment.

Lower the lure to a good depth and commence jigging, but wind in a few turns every so often, working the whole water column until you find the depth at which the fish are feeding. An alternative approach is to quickly wind in the rig back up to the surface. This doesn't give the fish any time to inspect the lures, and he just may throw caution to the wind and go for it before his chance is lost.

More durable than mackerel feathers, these are very effective when jigged.

If it's small fish like mackerel, herring, sardines or baitfish for your trolling line you're after, you'll need to scale down the pirk rig with a more appropriately sized set of lures. Replace the pirk with a small metal jig, as a large pirk will scare off the very fish that you're trying to catch. A small Yo-Zuri 'Hydro Metal' or 'Lil Jack' jig is ideal for this. The ubiquitous shop-bought strings of feathers can be used, but they're seldom well made enough to last long. Small hokkai lures, or similar by Fladen or Power Storm resembling tiny fish or shrimp are, in my view, more effective than traditional mackerel feathers and are more durable. Or you can make your own, using florists' ribbon and tinsel instead of real feathers. The best colours are red, white or black.

These 'feathers' shouldn't be too long, or the fish, rather unsportingly, strikes at the end of the feather rather than further up where the hook is. If necessary, trim them to within 20mm of the hook.

Multi-lured rigs like these can be a liability in the cockpit. It's all too easy to impale yourself on one hook while trying to deal with a lively fish on another.

Two lures, or at the most three, plus the pirk if used are about right.

But why wait until you're becalmed? If you spot an area of broken ground on the chart where demersal fish are likely to congregate, or an area off a headland where mackerel are known to shoal, it might pay to drop the sails and drift over those productive waters for a while.

TROPICAL AND SUB-TROPICAL OFFSHORE WATERS

If you have been barely moving through the water for an hour or two, you may well have attracted fish to the vicinity of your boat. The tendency of fish to congregate under floating objects is well known, and is used to good effect by local fisherman throughout the tropics. Not only do they utilise natural flotsam and jetsam, but they also rig some up themselves. In the West Indies local fishermen tie bundles of banana plant leaves together for this purpose. Off soundings they're left to drift, but if depth permits they're anchored to the seabed. The fishermen drift down onto these 'fish aggregation devices' (or FADs as they're known) and handline a baited hook in close proximity to catch the fish below them. The first time we came across a commercial FAD was off the Portuguese coast, when what appeared to be a submarine on the surface materialised on the horizon. As we got closer we could see it was a large raft-like structure, but neither Mary nor I could decide what it was. It wasn't charted and there was no sign of lights on it, so we were both very relieved that we found it in daylight. Only some time afterwards, in discussion with other cruisers, did we come to the conclusion that it was most likely a large FAD. But I digress – the point that I'm trying to make is that your nearly stationary yacht has become a FAD and is likely to have its own attendant fish population.

This is particularly good news for anyone unfortunate enough to find himself in a liferaft. These don't always have a fishing kit in their survival pack, so the inclusion of a few carefully selected lures in your grab bag is a very good idea.

A Baited Hook

First, have a look over the transom. See any fish lurking under the stern? If so, try a free-lined baited hook for them. A piece of an earlier catch retrieved from the fridge should do the trick. Watching a large fish as it decides whether or not to take your offering always gets the blood pumping through the arteries nicely. If the boat is moving at all you may need to take the baited hook forward and drop it near the bow so that it arrives at the stern at the same level as the attendant fish. If you're doubly fortunate in being offshore in tropical waters and really being smiled upon from above, a sacrificial flying fish will present itself on deck. Becalmed, it's best used alive. Let the live bait swim naturally away from the boat, giving it just enough line to avoid dragging it through the water. When the live bait starts to panic, prepare yourself for a strike. If, more likely, you've done nothing in your recent past to earn the flying fish, you'll need to resort to 'jigging' an artificial lure. The largest Dexter Wedge would be just the thing.

With a number of crew on deck, I would resist the temptation to try spinning from a drifting boat. This technique involves casting a small lure some distance away from the boat, then reeling it back in. Spinning and sailing boats aren't made for each other. In my experience more time is spent in unhooking the lure from the backstay/mainsheet/guard wires/sheets, some part of your own anatomy and more than once from that of a bitterly complaining crew, than ever from a fish's mouth. It's best left for the anchorage in my view.

AT ANCHOR

Arriving at their destination, trolling gear stowed away, many cruising skippers abandon all thoughts of fishing until their next offshore passage. Which is a shame, as they're missing out on a deal of low cost entertainment and some great fresh seafood.

Several proven fish-catching methods await you, including:

- **Bottom fishing**
- **Float fishing**
- **Spinning**
- **Jigging**
- **Light trolling from the tender**

But before you drop the hook, have a closer look at the large-scale chart of the anchorage. Is it possible to position the yacht over, or close to, a patch of rough ground where fish are likely to congregate? What other bottom features are nearby that could benefit you? A channel maybe, or a steep drop-off?

Dawn and dusk are again the most productive times, and light tackle gets the best results.

What's Down There?

In temperate waters your catch could include mackerel, garfish, mullet, bass, codling, whiting, pouting, bream, eels, pollack, flatfish, dogfish, wrasse, gurnard, skate, rays, squid, cuttlefish and octopus.

In tropical and subtropical seas, snapper, grunts, mackerel, porgies, jacks, snook, hinds, skate, rays, squid, cuttlefish and octopus will be your quarry. My advice, particularly in tropical waters, is not to mess with skates and rays – some of these being well-equipped to deliver nasty injuries and electric shocks. I suggest you cut your line as close to the hook as you safely can, and let the fish go. If intentionally leaving the hook in the fish's mouth offends you, flatten the barb with a pair of pliers before you start fishing. The fish will then have little difficulty in ridding itself of the hook.

The tender is your friend – it'll help you catch more fish. If the water is clear, don the polarising shades and make an exploratory trip around the anchorage when the sun is high to discover any rocky outcrops or other fish-holding grounds. As all coral-hoppers know, keep the sun over your shoulder or you'll see nothing but surface reflection. Alternatively you could use a clear-view bucket.

For bottom fishing and float fishing you'll need to bait the hook, but for spinning, jigging and trolling, a selection of lures is all you need. You'll need a rod and reel for float fishing and spinning, and although you can get by with a handline for bottom fishing, jigging and trolling I prefer to use the rod for these too. One lightish rod of around 8ft long and a medium sized fixed-spool reel will be fine.

Fixed-spool reels are normally sold with two spools. Load one with say, 8lb to 10lb monofilament line, and the other with around 20lb breaking strain line. See page 78 for advice on loading a reel with line.

Bottom Fishing

Although a term sharing the same unfortunate ambiguity as fly-fishing, bottom fishing should correctly suggest to you that it involves fishing on or close to the seabed. A two or three hook 'paternoster' is what you need to catch fish that feed on or just clear of the bottom.

The weight should be just heavy enough to keep the rig on the bottom, and to enable you to maintain and 'feel' contact. A biting fish will pull against the weight, so the heavier the weight the more resistance the fish will feel, and the more likely it is to be spooked.

Bait the hooks with something fishy, more of which later, and lower the rig to the seabed.

Don't let the rocking of the boat cause the sinker to bounce repeatedly on the bottom, as the sonic vibrations will alarm the fish. If you use a handline you'll need to keep hold of it to feel the bites, unless you can seek out a well-intentioned fish that's prepared to hook itself. A rod can be used 'hands-free' providing a watchful eye is kept on its tip for signs of a bite.

If your rod holder is adjustable, change its offshore trolling position to around 75° from the vertical for bottom fishing. Left in the trolling position the angle between the line and the rod will be too acute for bite detection and any nibbling fish is likely to drop the bait on feeling the resistance of the rod.

You may find that the lower hook receives the constant attention of unwanted, and inedible shore crabs in which case you should shorten the lower dropper so that it's around 6 inches or so clear of the sea bed.

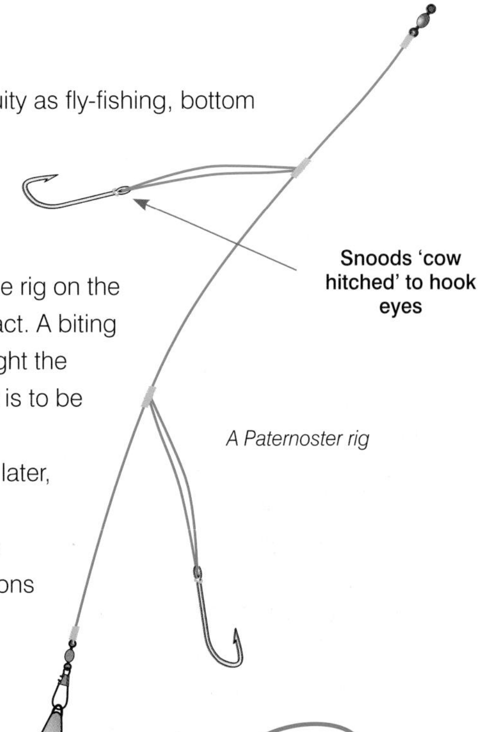

A Paternoster rig

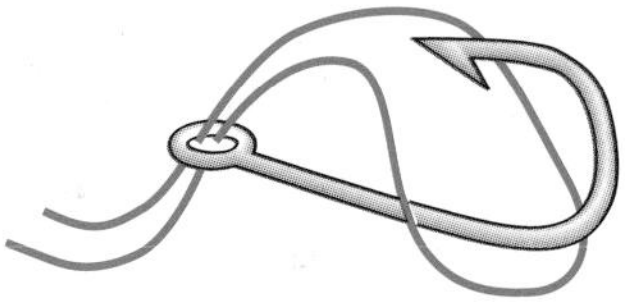

Attach the snood to the hook with a simple 'cow hitch'. Pass the loop through the eye, pass it over the hook, and pull tight.

At a pinch you could use your offshore trolling rod and reel with a very much lighter leader, but the rigidity of the rod will make bite detection difficult and the whole experience less pleasurable than with a lighter, more suitable outfit.

Whether you choose to use a handline or a rod, it's vital to keep the line fairly tight. If it goes slack, you'll lose contact with your hook and a fish will be off with your bait before you know it. This is probably the single most common reason for failing to catch fish at anchor.

Mary catches a nice pan-sized jack with a Jelly Baby jig set below hokkai shrimps. Sailors would envy the lack of overhead obstructions on this powerboat.

A worse scenario is that the fish will gulp the bait straight down and munch through your line. If the hook was stainless steel the fish is likely to suffer a slow and painful death with the hook embedded in its gut. For bait fishing I recommend that you use bronzed steel hooks instead of stainless ones. These are far more likely to be dissolved by the fish's digestive process, leaving it to bite and fight another day. You'll need to sharpen them more often, and ditch them when they become corroded, but they're much cheaper than stainless hooks.

A paternoster is fished as an up-and-down rig, that is, the line between the weight and the rod tip is vertical or thereabouts. If there's much current running through the anchorage the rig will swing off the bottom. Letting out more line won't help, and replacing the sinker with a heavier one will result in fewer bites. It's time to change your rig to a ledger.

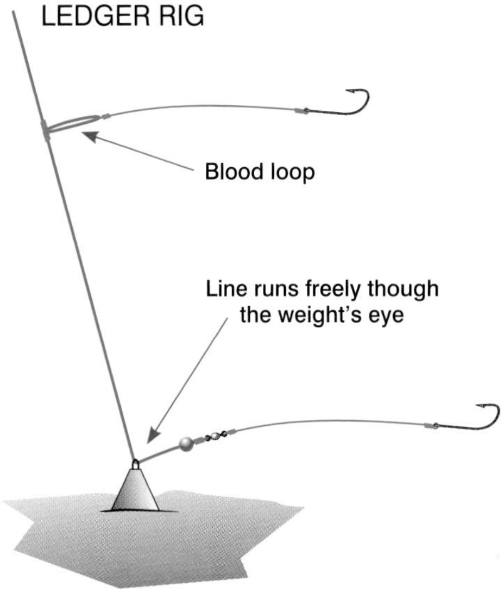

Now the size of the sinker can be increased sufficiently to hold bottom, as a biting fish draws the line through the lead and feels little resistance.

If the yacht is swinging on its anchor, or pitching or rolling, results will be poor as your bait will be dragged around in an unnatural manner and you'll be unable to maintain contact with your baited hook. Fishing over the transom as close to the boat's centreline as possible, rather than over the cockpit side, will reduce the rolling effect but not the swinging. Or you could try float tackle, and let it drift far enough away for it to be unaffected by the yacht's motion. Then, unfortunately, there'll probably be so much slack in the line that you'll only ever hook the most persistent fish. Maybe it's time to give the fish a break, and grab a beer and a good book.

We were anchored in Anse de Pitons in St Lucia. Shortly after dawn I had caught a couple of snapper around a pound and a half each, and was scaling them on 'Alacazam's sugar-scoop. A local fisherman I had met the previous day was motoring past. I called him over and poured us both a coffee. We chatted about our joint good fortune in finding ourselves in this fabulous location in the shadow of the spectacular Pitons, and then the conversation turned naturally to fish. He had clearly caught something as evidenced by the large red tail that poked out from beneath the banana leaves in the sole of his pirogue. Seven red snapper between around 12lb and 25lb apiece. Seeing my hanging jaw he explained his technique, which was simplicity itself – a handline, a large hook and a whole fresh mackerel hooked through the tail. Fishing on the drift in the very deep water a couple of miles offshore he just freelined the mackerel into the depths until he ran out of line or a fish took it. The technique clearly worked – seven times at least. My two tiddlers made a very nice lunch though.

TIP Groundbaiting, or 'chumming', can really produce the goods when fishing at anchor in this way. It'll need to, as it involves a raid on the galley store locker, which is unlikely to be supported wholeheartedly by your first mate. A successful raid will gain you a tin of tuna in oil and some bread. Mix the two ingredients together into a stiff paste, put it into a net bag with a sinker and suspend it just off the seabed. Give it a jiggle now and again to release food particles into the oil stream that will be ebbing from the bag. Fish will drawn to the food source, where they will pounce gratefully upon your baited hook. Your small investment is likely to be rewarded in spades.

FLOAT FISHING

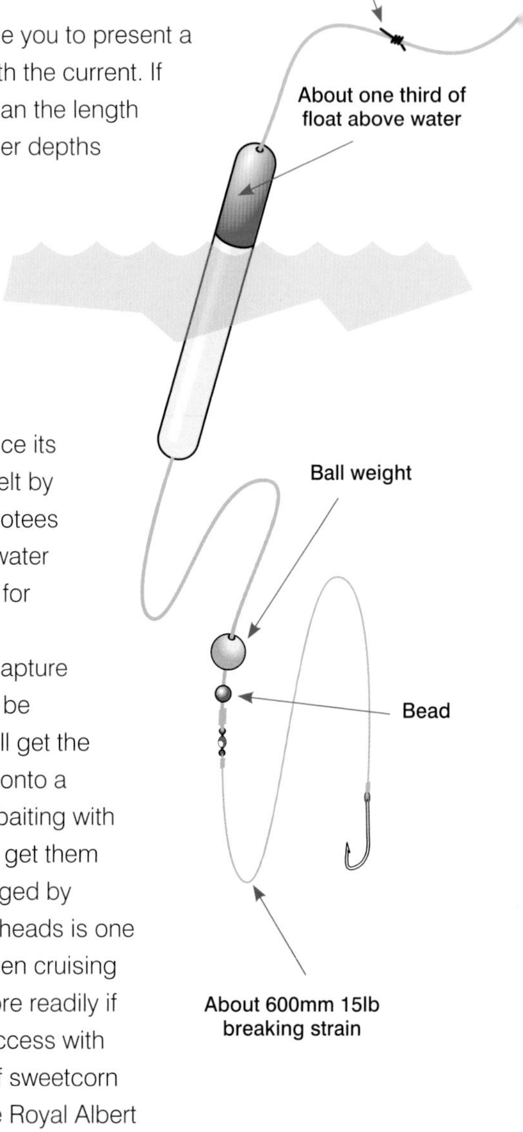

In more reasonable conditions, float fishing will enable you to present a bait above the bottom, where it can drift enticingly with the current. If you want to fish more than a couple of feet deeper than the length of the rod you'll need to use a sliding float rig. At lesser depths the float can be fixed at the appropriate position on the main line.

Floats come in a large number of shapes, sizes and colours. The larger and more buoyant the float the larger the bait that can be suspended under it, but more resistance will be felt by a biting fish. If you need a large float for reasons of visibility, using a larger weight will reduce its residual buoyancy and thus the effective resistance felt by the fish. Heavy and light displacement have their devotees – familiar ground for most sailors! As a lifelong freshwater angler, I can cheerfully watch a float bobbing around for hours.

Float fishing for grey mullet is great fun, but their capture is unlikely to raise a cheer from cooks. Mullet tend to be cautious fish, so light lines, small hooks and floats will get the best results. A small piece of bread lightly squeezed onto a size 12 hook will normally get their attention. Groundbaiting with soaked bread, squeezed into dense balls will help to get them feeding. Make sure the bread sinks, or you'll be mugged by hoards of gleeful gulls. Flushing the bread down the heads is one answer to this problem. Whilst mullet can often be seen cruising around on the surface, they seem to take the bait more readily if it's fished about 1½m to 2m down. I've had good success with mullet on Devon's River Tamar using a single grain of sweetcorn on a size 10 hook, at a spot conveniently close to the Royal Albert Bridge Inn. It's strange how they stop biting around opening time. In the UK, grey mullet aren't highly regarded from a gastronomic point of view. However, red mullet will definitely get the thumb's up and black and striped mullet are considered a delicacy along the gulf coasts of Alabama and northwest Florida. None of the mullet referred to here should be confused with the red mullet, a bottom feeding fish, which outside Europe are often (and less confusingly) called goatfish.

Spinning

Spinning, as briefly referred to earlier, means casting a lure some distance, then winding it back in, rather like trolling over a short distance from a stationary position. It's so named because early lures were designed to rotate, causing vibrations in the water, and these 'spinners' are still widely used to great effect. Many modern casting lures don't spin at all and are often interchangeable with those used for trolling: spoons, jigs and plugs. When cast, a varied rate of retrieve will cause them to rise and fall, imitating the distressed action of a wounded fish – an easy meal for a hungry predator.

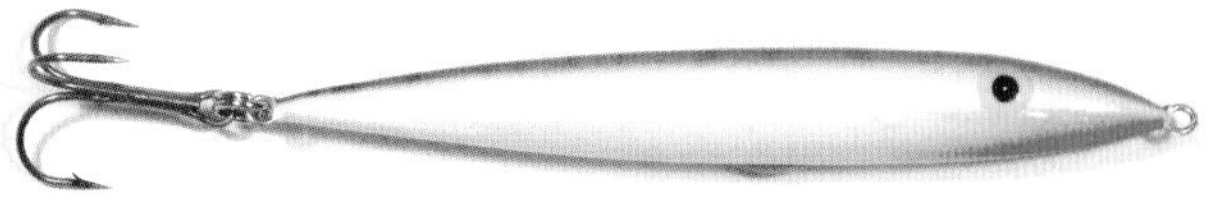

Casting lures come with different characteristics. The top one here is heavy and will sink, whereas the one below is designed to skitter along the surface.

Spinning is more proactive than trolling. You can cast your lure to where you think the fish are likely to be, choose a specific depth, vary its rate of retrieve and, to some extent, change its direction. For this task, a fixed spool reel - it needn't be a large one - is much easier to control than a multiplier.

Trot along to your local tackle shop and take a look at the lures on display. It's likely to leave you bewildered, but console yourself with the knowledge that many of them are designed primarily to catch the angler, not fish. I should know. I've ended up with lots.

Bucktail lures are often fished using a 'sink-and-draw' technique. This involves casting the lure and letting it sink to the bottom. Then lift the rod tip, winding in a few turns and dropping the rod tip as you do so. Let the lure sink to the bottom again and repeat the process until you get a take or the lure is fully retrieved. Fish often take just as the lure is lifted off the bottom. Bucktail lures are often used with a strip squid or fish on the hook.

A small fixed spool reel is great for fishing at anchor

As discussed previously, some plugs are designed to float on the surface until you start to reel them in. Then a steel vane at the forward end of the lure provides enough downward force to overcome their buoyancy. The faster you wind the deeper they dive. They're particularly useful when fishing in shallow water over rocks and coral outcrops, where by slowing the rate of retrieve you can allow the lure to rise in the water and avoid getting snagged.

Sinking lures – how fast?

If you're casting a sinking lure, it's very useful to know how fast it sinks. Some manufacturers print the rate of sinking on the lure's packaging, but for those that don't it's simple to find it out. Choose a calm day at anchor, and drop the lure over the side making sure that the line's slack enough to allow it to sink naturally. Count the seconds between it hitting the surface and it's arrival on the seabed, which you can tell by watching the line at the surface as it follows the lure down. Now check the depth on the depth sounder making due allowance for any keel offset, divide the depth by the time and you'll know the lure's sinking rate.

Spinning from a tender

Then, when using it from the tender, by counting off the seconds following the lure hitting the surface you'll know the approximate depth of the lure when you start your retrieve. Search for fish at various depths. When you get a strike, focus on at that level for at least the next few casts. Vary the speed of retrieve; try short sprints followed by a period of steady winding. Then stop for a few seconds to allow the lure to sink deeper, and move the rod from side to side to change its direction. Remember that you're trying to imitate the action of a small, injured and frightened fish, separated from the relative safety of its shoal.

OF PLUGS AND FLIES

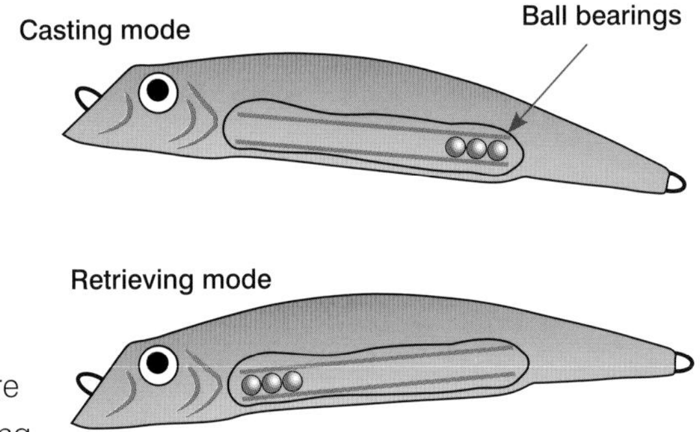

The ball bearings are contained in an internal channel. When the lure hits the water they roll forward to improve the swimming action.

There's another type of plug that's designed specifically for casting. These are known as 'suspending' types and have neutral buoyancy. On retrieve they dive to a depth and stay at that depth irrespective of the rate of retrieve. They're designed to imitate an injured fish, darting around under a fast retrieve, then fluttering and rolling to a stop without sinking or rising when you stop winding in. It's when in this motionless state, suspended in mid-water that most strikes occur. They're great fun to use and can be devastating fish catchers. Try a retrieve, twitch, pause, twitch, retrieve sequence, the twitch being made with the rod tip.

Some plug manufacturers incorporate loose weights inside the lure that locates at the back end of the plug during casting and improves distance and accuracy in flight. However, a lure so weighted would have a poor swimming action and catch few fish as a result. So to overcome this failing, an internal magnet pulls back the weight into its designed location once the energy of the cast is depleted. Clever stuff.

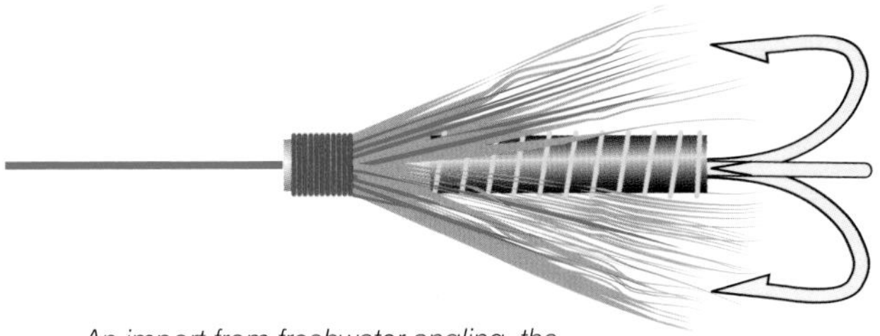
An import from freshwater angling, the tube-fly is just as effective afloat

One other small casting lure that we haven't so far mentioned is the tube-fly. Unlike other fly-type designs where the fly is tied around the shank of the hook, tube-fly design locates the hook, often a treble, right aft where short-striking fish are less likely to miss it. The 'fly', intended to resemble a small fish or shrimp, is tied around a plastic tube, such as the depleted innards of a ball-point pen. They're simple to make, and as the body is made up without a hook, manufacture can be left safely in the hands of your offspring. Tube-flies were developed 50-odd years ago primarily for freshwater salmon and trout fishing, but are just as effective for other saltwater species. They are traditionally used with fly fishing tackle, but not having any of that aboard – you have to stop somewhere – I use light spinning gear. A couple of lead split-shot are squeezed onto the line about 1m ahead of the fly to enable casting and getting it to sink. I fish these by twitching them along a few inches at a time just above the bottom, and get best results in shallow water over sea-grass.

Little to do with catching fish is ever a certainty, but if you find yourself in the cockpit with a spinning rod when a shoal of baitfish erupts from the surface within casting distance, then you're at least in with a very good chance. Just cast your lure to the far side of the melee and retrieve. The strike will probably be spectacular. Only if you have a small livebait to hand is your success likely to be more assured.

JIGGING FOR CEPHALOPODS

Jigging can be done from the cockpit of an anchored yacht, but it's best done from a drifting tender simply because you'll cover more ground. Other than to scale your lure sizes down to suit the size of the fish you hope to catch, there's little more to be said about it than was said previously. Except that is, for jigging for cephalopods, which include squid, cuttlefish and octopus. They all share at least two attributes – tentacles and ink, both of which they'll use to the disadvantage of those who catch them. When caught, they're best left in a keepnet over the side for a while where they can discharge their tanks at will. Even so a well-aimed jet will get you sooner or later, so leave the nice white sweater your auntie gave you for your birthday back on the boat.

Squid eat small fish and shrimp, and hunt for these around seaweed and kelp mainly during the hours of darkness. Somewhat perversely, they prefer some light amongst their darkness. But they seem to be completely put off feeding if there's anything more than a gentle breeze ruffling the surface. So choose a calm night, find a weedy bottom close to a well-lit jetty and you're likely to be squids in.

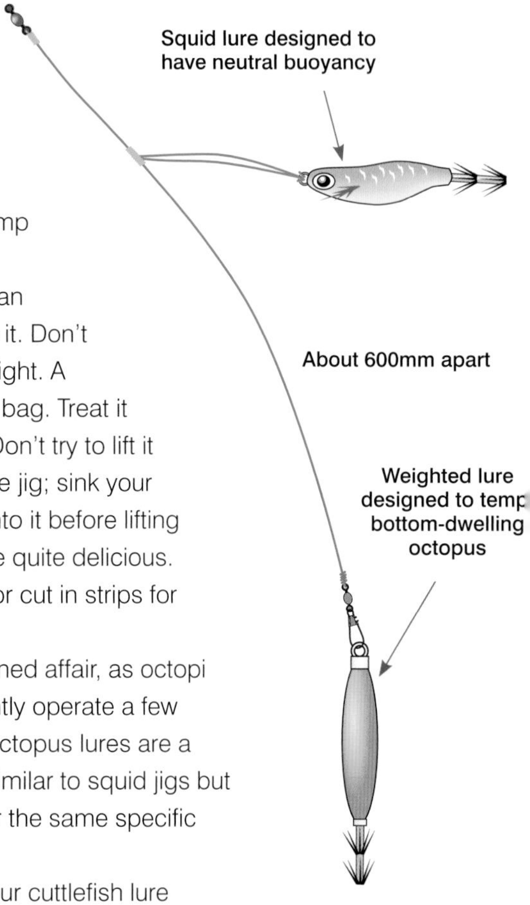

The only new equipment you'll need is a small selection of specialised squid jigs. These sinking lures are almost exclusively imitation shrimps and are produced in a variety of colours. I've had best success with pink ones, which may lead you to conclude that squid prefer their shrimp cooked. Luminous versions are worth a try too.

Fish the jig close to the weedy bottom and give it an occasional twitch of the rod tip as you slowly retrieve it. Don't expect a reel-screaming run and an arm-wrenching fight. A hooked squid feels like a marginally energetic paper bag. Treat it like one, and continue to reel in gently or it'll fall off. Don't try to lift it out of the water, expecting it to hang on gamely to the jig; sink your landing net under the surface and draw your squid into it before lifting inboard. Squid are easy to prepare and cook and are quite delicious. They also make fine bait, either whole for larger fish or cut in strips for smaller ones.

Fishing for cuttlefish and octopus can be a combined affair, as octopi skulk around on the seabed and cuttlefish conveniently operate a few inches above. The lures are quite different though. Octopus lures are a weighted grapnel-like affair. Cuttlefish lures appear similar to squid jigs but neither sink nor float. They have neutral buoyancy (or the same specific gravity as seawater).

Rig the octopus lure at the end of your line and your cuttlefish lure about 18" above on a short snood. A pal of mine has had great success with this rig in the Culatra anchorage on the Portuguese Algarve. If you wish to catch cuttlefish but not octopus, replace the octopus lure with a lead sinker. Unlike squid, cuttlefish and octopus feed in broad daylight. They're easy to catch and delicious to eat.

USING THE TENDER

Trolling inshore from the tender is pretty much the same as from the yacht, except that you'll probably be using lighter tackle and smaller lures. If you're using a rod, it may be worth buying a rod holder that clamps to the tender's transom. Again, secure the rod with a lanyard to a convenient strong point.

Seek out those places likely to hold fish, such as over any kind of rough ground and around headlands, along drop-offs and the edge of currents or tidal eddies. In shallow water row the tender rather than firing-up the outboard or you'll disturb both other cruisers and the fish alike. Pass either astern or well ahead of other anchored yachts, or you'll risk the embarrassment of hooking up their anchor chains.

My favourite method is a mixture of trolling and jigging, 'jigolling' as I call it. Using either a bucktail jig or a soft plastic lure far enough astern to be bouncing along the seabed, raise and lower the rod with a twitching action. On both of these lure types the hook is on the top of the lure, reducing the tendency to catch in weed. However, if you do get weeded-up or snag the bottom, connect a 3-way swivel about 1.5m ahead of the lure and suspend a lead weight on a weaker line length about 600mm below the swivel. The weight should be no heavier than required to keep just in touch with the seabed. If there's sufficient wind or current to move you slowly along, that's perfect as you will be able to hold the rod. Otherwise, leave the rod in the rod holder and row sporadically. An evening or early morning spent so in a tranquil Caribbean anchorage is paradise itself, and has brought many tasty fish to 'Alacazam's galley.

There's much to be said for having a small telescopic rod on board, and using it to troll a lure when returning from a trip ashore in the tender. It'll be small enough when collapsed to fit inside a shoulder bag, and may well pay for itself many times over.

If the seabed is sand or shingle there may well be flatfish about. These fish – plaice, flounders, dabs and sole (and turbot and brill if you're exceptionally fortunate) – feed on a diet of marine worms and small fish, and can be caught from an anchored boat or a slowly drifting tender. Drifting enables you to cover more ground, but it's important that the movement of your bait on the seabed isn't greatly different in terms of speed and direction from the other morsels that are drifting around in the current down there. So drifting in calm conditions will be most productive. Try using a strip of squid or fresh oily fish on the hook. A spoon a few inches up from the hook will bring the flatfish's attention to bait that follows behind it, and a dropper around 18" above the sinker will pick up any other more rotund species that may be around. If you drift into an area of broken ground you're almost certain to get hung up, so hang on to your rod.

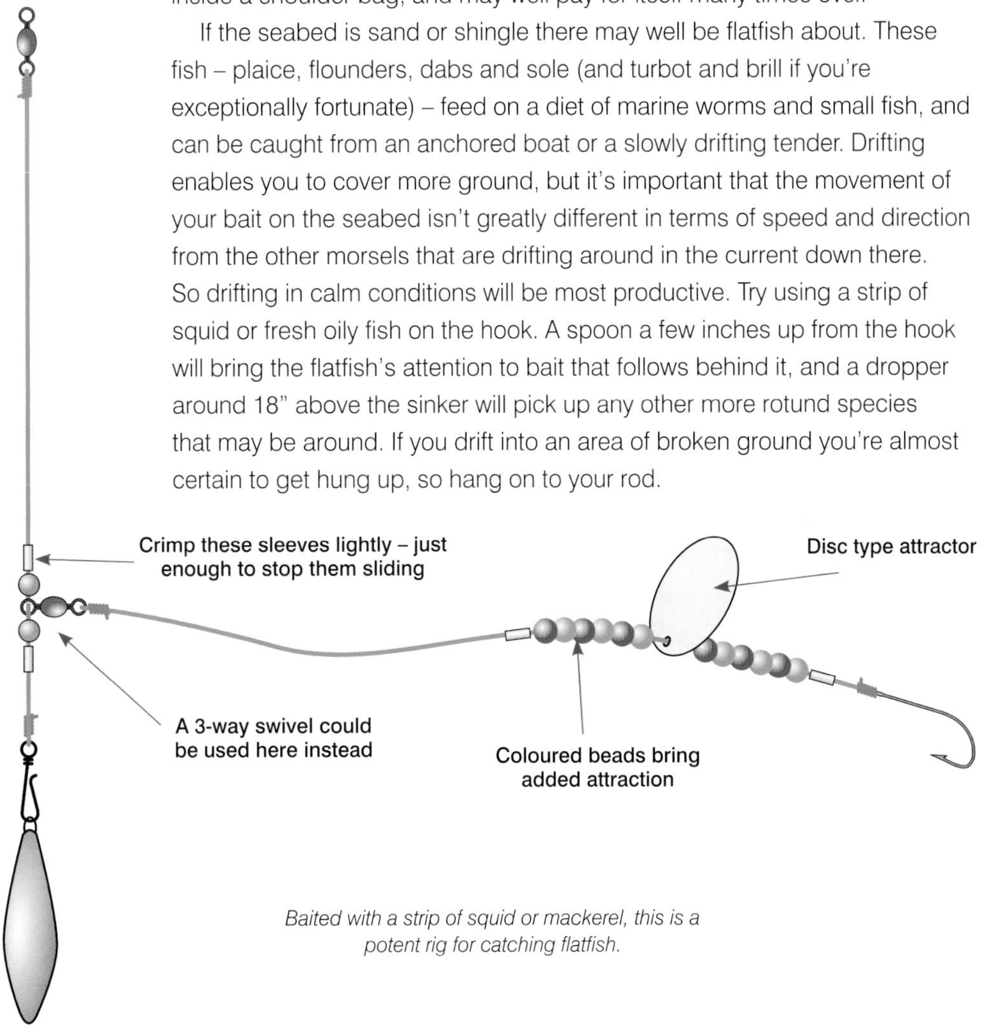

Baited with a strip of squid or mackerel, this is a potent rig for catching flatfish.

TANGLE NETS

If you're anchored over broken ground, there could be a crab or lobster prowling around below. You may wish to try a tangle net. This is nothing more than a section of discarded monofilament gill net that, sadly, can be found washed up on many of the world's shores. Many commercial fishermen use these nets, as they're cheap, rot free and very effective. But they're almost invisible to fish and other sea creatures, so when they get caught up on a rock outcrop or a wreck, they continue to trap anything that swims long after the fishing boat has abandoned them. Divers have told me of wrecks cocooned in a shroud of rotting fish as a result. Along with the illegal longline fishermen of the Southern Ocean, who accept as collateral damage the deaths of more than 100,000 albatross that swallow their squid baited hooks each year, they show callous disregard for the world's wildlife.

So if you find a section of this dreadful stuff and choose to use it, tie a chunk of fish in the centre of it and lower it to the bottom on a length of cord. Leave it there overnight, and retrieve it the following morning. If you're lucky you'll find a crab or lobster entangled in it. When you no longer need the net, burn it. Otherwise it may end up on a landfill site where it'll ensnare birds just as effectively as its intended victims.

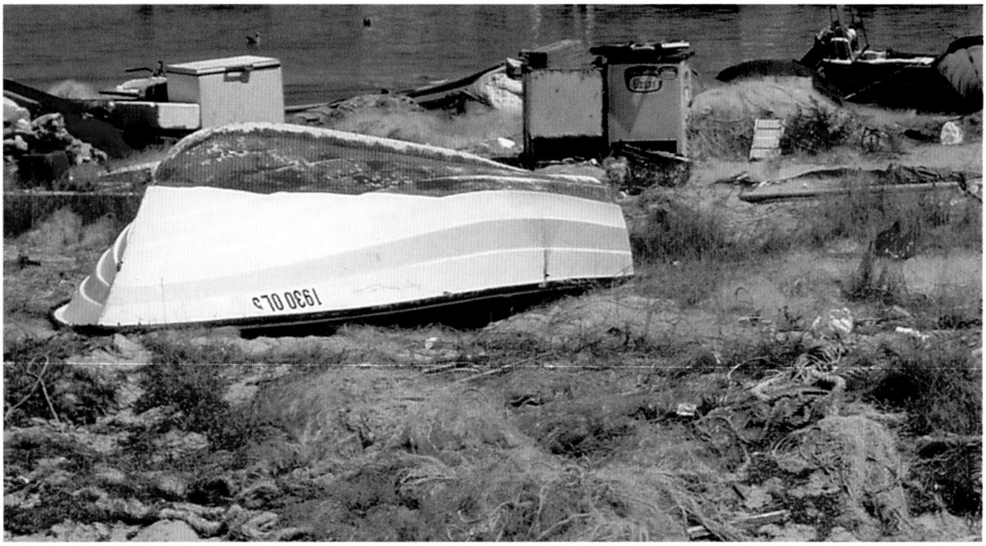

Discarded nets are a menace to wildlife, both ashore and underwater.

IN THE MARINA

Holed-up in a marina while gales rage outside can be a frustrating (and expensive) experience, but I console myself with the thought that it's better to be in a marina wishing you were outside, than being out there wishing you were tucked up inside. But even tied up alongside in a marina there're opportunities to catch fish, particularly school bass and mullet in European waters using light float tackle as previously described, or a paternoster gear dropped close to a pile. And it's here that the younger members of the crew will develop an initial curiosity for marine creatures, possibly leading to a lifelong interest of this fascinating world.

For many offspring of seafaring parents, this is where they will serve their apprenticeship in the noble art of crabbing. A piece of fish or meat (bacon is a favourite) tied to a length of weighted twine fished on the bottom will keep them occupied for hours. Not to be confused with edible crab, the local shore crabs enter into the spirit of it with a deal of enthusiasm. Some years ago, having tied up my Nicholson 32 'Jalingo 2' alongside the pontoon at Audierne in France, I had left my young children James and Samantha handlining from the cockpit while I plundered the nearby supermarket. In my absence they experienced the suicidal shore crab phenomena, and caught half a bucketful in about twenty minutes. Knowing my predilection for seafood, they cooked the lot and presented me with a bowlful of the little green chaps on my return. To this day they miss few opportunities to remind me of my ungrateful reaction.

Bass love live shrimp, and these often reside in the weed growth on the piles that support the pontoon. A gentle upward scrape with a fishing net will dislodge them. Use a small freshwater hook of no more than size 12 (or you're likely to kill the shrimp which makes it much less attractive), and light float tackle.

Local Fishing Regulations

Before fishing in any country's national waters for the first time, check local regulations. You may need a permit, or, some specific methods such as the tangle net described above, may be illegal. Many isolated communities depend on their local fish stocks, and rightly guard them jealously. In some parts of the world ignorance of the fishing laws could even get your boat confiscated, and you and your crew imprisoned. A good time to find out about local regulations is when clearing customs and immigration. But if fishing is permitted and you make a good catch, you should never try and sell it ashore. Distribute it quietly amongst your fellow cruisers, or better still give it to the locals. If you try to sell it, not only are you taking their fish you're stealing their livelihood as well. It won't be appreciated. This is particularly true when fishing in the anchorage, where your success is likely to occur under the gaze of the locals, many of whom will be fishermen themselves.

In the West Indies, we often find our first contact with the locals is through the fishermen. A gift of a few hooks, or a lure, and a chat over a couple of cool beers goes a long way to ensuring a warm and lasting welcome ashore – and there's a good chance that you'll learn the location of the local fishing hotspots.

BAIT

Bait can be purchased from specialised bait shops, or from regular shops and supermarkets. The former will deal in live bait such as worms, sand eels and peeler crabs, whilst the latter will provide you with refrigerated and frozen fish products intended for human consumption. Alternatively you can collect your own, but as with fishing in territorial waters, local regulations must be checked before you set about any kind of bait collection. In many areas there are restrictions, and in others you may need a licence. In the worst case, if you're found to have inadvertently collected a protected species, the resulting fine you may also collect can be enormous. Whilst many sea anglers rate live marine worms as the prime bait, harvesting them involves a deal of digging in glutinous mud with a long-pronged gardening fork. I'm guessing that you have neither the inclination nor the necessary equipment aboard.

But you should be able to get hold of some of the following:

- **Live shrimp and small live fish, by catching it yourself**
- **Fresh squid, by catching it yourself**
- **Frozen squid, from shoreside shops and supermarkets**
- **Fresh, frozen and cooked shrimp, from shoreside shops and supermarkets**
- **Fresh sprat or ballyhoo, from shoreside shops and supermarkets or a local fisherman**
- **Shellfish, by collecting it yourself.**

Live bait is probably most effective, followed by fresh fish or shrimp, then frozen squid and cooked shrimp. Whichever you use, it's most important to hook them correctly. When using the uni-knot, or a crimped connection to attach a hook for strip baits like fish and squid, leave the lazy end about 15mm long to help retain the bait.

A drop net is very useful for catching live shrimps and prawns for bait – or the pan. Bait it with a chunk of fish and suspend it from the transom, close to the bottom. It needs to hang vertically in the water to get results, so use it at slack water or where there's little current.

Or you can use a fish trap, but again it won't perform if it's dragged around the seabed by a yacht swinging on its anchor. I unashamedly admit to spending many a contented hour scraping around in knee deep water with a shrimp net, confirming my beloved's belief that I haven't properly grown up yet.

Fish trap. Not as bulky as it looks. It concertinas into an almost flat disc.

This is a great way of collecting small fish and shrimp, but always wear something on your feet to provide protection from sharp objects and the poisonous spines of weaver fish and their more toxic tropical cousin, the stonefish. Just push the net along in front of you, using the wooden edge of the net to lightly scrape the seabed and disturb the residents.

It was while poking around with a shrimp net along the shore of True Blue Bay in Grenada that I met Tino, a local angler. A discussion on bait collection ensued.

"Ever tried a cast net?" he asked.

"No" I replied.

"You get one and I'll get my pal to teach you" said Tino.

The following day I trotted down to Island Water World in St Georges, and bought one. True to his word, Tino's pal spent an afternoon trying to show me how to throw the thing. It's not easy and takes a lot of practice to get it right. Once mastered however, it's a great way of catching small fish and shrimp, either from the shore or from the dinghy.

Shellfish

Shellfish are generally one of two types – those that attach themselves to rocks and those that live in the sand. In temperate seas, mussels can be found on any submerged structure or densely clumped together in muscle beds attached to rocks. They thrive in areas protected from breaking waves. The bait is, of course, inside the shell, which you can safely open with a blunt knife. Elastic thread can be used to secure this delicate bait on the hook. On the rocks you'll probably also find limpets. These conically shaped shellfish exist cheerfully on even the most wave-battered rock, and are extremely reluctant to let go of it. Hence their success, I suppose, but a blade slid under the edge of the shell will eventually do the trick. Once removed, don't put them back on the rock or you'll have to go through the whole process again.

Cockles live in sand, close to the low-water line. They're equally as good bait as a mussel, but have two advantages. You don't need a knife to open them. Just put them back-to-back so the knuckles interlock, and twist. One of them will open. They're also much tougher than mussels and stay on the hook better. If you put a mussel on the hook first, then the cockle, the mussel won't fall off. This is known somewhat poetically as a cockle/mussel cocktail.

Whilst cockle hunting you may see an occasional squirt of water erupt from a small oval-shaped depression in the sand. This is caused by the aptly named razorshell, which is in residence below. Not only do they look like an old cut-throat razor but the edge of their shell is almost as sharp, so handle them with care. Now here's a trick – sprinkle some salt into the depression which will fool it into thinking the tide's come in, whereupon it will rise, phoenix like, from the sand. Grab it before it realises your cruel deception, apply gentle pressure and you'll feel it release its grip. Don't let go until you've got it clear of the sand or it will shoot back down again, and a whole bucketful of salt won't entice it to re-emerge. Open the shell and thread the flesh onto the hook. It's tough enough to stay there on its own.

For all shellfish use a fine-wire hook such as the Mustad Aberdeen.

CHAPTER 4

Making the right connections

Fish are lost for a number of reasons but high on the list of causes are inappropriate hooks and swivels and poorly made connections. Compared to the rest of your kit, the hardware involved is extremely inexpensive so there's really no excuse.

Inexpensive maybe, but don't buy cheap. Only use good quality hooks and swivels from reputable manufacturers. I tend to go for Mustad hooks and either Mustad or Berkley swivels, but hooks made by Maruto, Gamakatsu and Miriabu and swivels by Sampro and Spro are of very similar quality.

Loading reels

It's important to avoid winding on twists. To load a centrepin or multiplier, attach the line from the line spool to the reel drum with a uni-knot, push a pencil or similar spindle through the centre of the line spool and wind away on the reel allowing the line spool to rotate. Distribute the line evenly back and forth across the reel drum with your thumb.

A fixed spool reel can't be loaded with line in the same way as for a multiplier, or the line will twist and tangles will develop as the line comes off the reels. To avoid this, the line must be wound off the edge of the line spool without allowing it to rotate. If twists still develop, turn the line spool over and allow the line to spill off from the other side.

Hooks

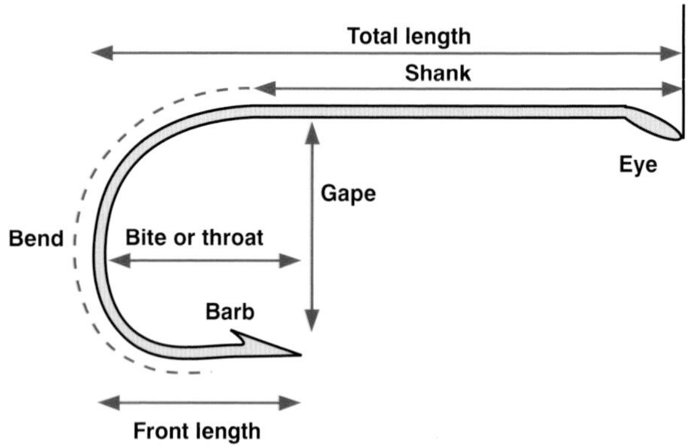

These come in a vast array of sizes and patterns. They range in size from size 32 for the tiniest freshwater dry fly, to an enormous 19/0 for the largest shark rig. You'll need nothing smaller than a size 12 freshwater hook for mullet or larger than a 10/0 for tuna.

There are three basic types – singles, doubles and trebles. Some hooks have an offset, or reversed, point which is supposed to improve their penetration capabilities. These are fine for bait but unsuitable for lures, as the twist in the hook may cause the lure to spin or run offline. The Mustad Sea Master is an example of this type.

The shank of the hook is the straight part, and is referred to as either being short, regular or long. Short shank hooks are used where you want to hide it inside the bait, and long shanks where your want to get more bait on. Regular shanks are pretty much for anything else.

For maximum hook strength look for those that have closed brazed eyes rather than those with the eye open – that's to say just bent around and butted up to the shank.

For offshore trolling lures you won't go far wrong by using Mustad's 'Southern & Tuna' or 'Sea Demon' patterns. These have knife edge points, the two ground sides of which can be easily sharpened with a whetstone or file. The inner surface of the barb is flat, thus making it difficult for a large fish to throw the hook. There's one hook pattern that looks as though it belongs in the manufacturer's reject bin. This, the circle hook (see right), with its turned-in point looks incapable of hooking anything, but the principle behind it is elegantly simple. Once the fish has swallowed the hook, and the angler applies tension to the line, the hook is dragged harmlessly from the fish's stomach until it enters the mouth where its design causes it to embed itself in the corner of the fish's mouth. For 'catch-and-release' billfish anglers the benefits are obvious, as the risk of gut-hooking a fish are greatly reduced and unhooking can be done simply and quickly with no damage to these impressive creatures (the fish, not the anglers). Circle hooks are used when nose-rigging bait fish, in conjunction with the drop-back technique.

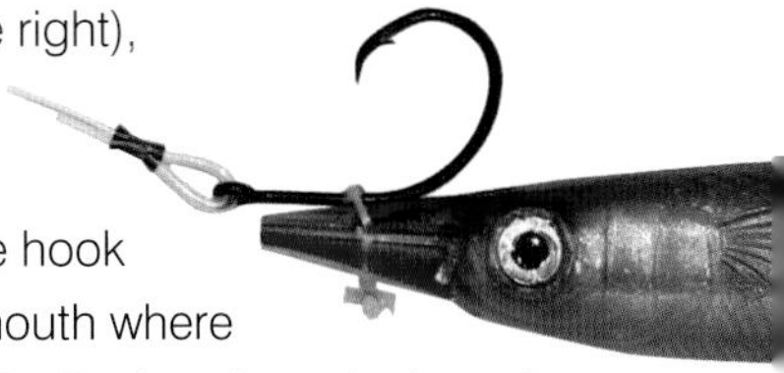

Hook sizes

It's easy to become confused with hook sizes. Those designated thus – 3/0, 4/0, 5/0 etc – embrace larger hooks where the size increases with the number. Smaller hooks use numbers without the /0. For this group the hook size decreases as the number increases. That's to say a size 4 hook will be smaller than a size 3 hook.

Simple? Not really but you soon get the hang of it.

As described earlier many anglers have reservations about the treble hooks often found on shop-bought lures and prefer to replace them with singles or doubles like Mustad's Dublin Point hook.

Skirted lures, particularly the larger ones in your collection can benefit by having the single hook replaced by a pair of single hooks rigged in tandem and orientated at 90° to each other. They are fixed in this position either by using heat shrink tubing or self-amalgamating tape.

Specialist hooks include those with sliced shanks, which are for two or more barbs intended to prevent shellfish and fish baits from sliding round into the bend of the hook. Hooks are made in either plain carbon steel, which corrodes in seawater, or stainless steel which doesn't. As a result the plain carbon hooks need to be sharpened more often than stainless, rinsed in freshwater and dried at the end of each trip to prevent them rusting.

However, there's a body of opinion which says that ordinary steel hooks are more humane since any fish that escapes with one inside will soon get shot of it when the hooks corrode – a process accelerated by digestive juices. Hmm, well maybe. Conversely, the less charitable amongst us reckon that any fish making off with one of our expensive lures deserves some discomfort for a while. The decision is for you and your conscience.

Swivels

Two ball bearing swivel designs. The 'Aussie' swivel on the left can be wound through rod guides.

Without these, your rig will become impossible to use. The line will twist, kink and eventually break. Your lure won't operate properly and coils of line will jam in your reel and rod rings. They're produced in one of two colours – silver or black. When trolling for large species I'd advise against using silver ones, since the fish might snap at the wrong thing and bite through the line. When after smaller species – mackerel or bass for example – the opposite is true as anything that attracts the fish to the vicinity of your lure is welcomed.

There are three basic types – plain swivels, snap swivels and three-way swivels – and two designs – barrel or ball-bearing. They're available in various sizes in breaking strains from 20lb to 275lb. Ball bearing swivels continue to operate effectively at very high loads, whereas a barrel swivel might not. Clearly, ball bearing swivels are the better option but they're considerably more expensive than their inferior cousins. My advice, particularly for offshore trolling, is to go for the ball bearing versions.

There is one other type of swivel – the Aussie swivel. These extra heavy duty swivels originally found favour with Australian crews hunting the giant Black Marlin on the Great Barrier reef. They have a reputation as being the strongest in the world, with breaking strains of up to 1,000lb. You won't need any of these, but a smaller version known as a Pro-rigger Wind-on Aussie swivel may be very useful when using a rod for trolling. These amazing swivels have a breaking strain of 200lb (90kg) yet are only 4 mm in diameter so you may be able to wind right them through your rod guides and onto your reel.

Connecting the Hardware

There are three places you'll need to make a connection:

- **Between main line and leader**
- **At a swivel**
- **At the hook (or lure)**

Provided your mono is not more than about 150lb breaking strain, a knot will be perfectly adequate for these. But for heavier mono leaders you'll find it impossible to cinch the knots up tight, and will need to make a crimped connection.

Although it's convenient to use a link swivel at the line to lure connection, it might impede the action of the lure. So I use the Rapala knot or a crimped connection for this.

KNOTS

The required properties of sailors' knots are that they're reliable under load and are easy to undo. Unfortunately, none of them work well in mono; they either slip or break. You'll need to learn a few new ones.

All knots reduce the strength of the line they're tied in, thereby becoming the weakest link in your rig. Specialised knots have been developed for us fishermen which reduce our rig strengths least.

The best include these:

Uni-knot Use it for tying monofilament to hooks or swivels, or, as a double uni-knot, main line to a monofilament leader. (see page 82)

Braid knot Use it for tying braid to swivels. (see page 82)

Snood knot Use it for tying monofilament to hooks with a turned-up or turned-down eye, and tandem hook rigs. (see page 82)

Blood loop Use it for droppers. (see page 83)

Albright Special Use it for tying monofilament or braid to single strand wire. (see page 83)

Haywire twist Use it for tying single strand wire to hooks and swivels. (see page 84)

Flemish eye Use it to create a reinforced loop in a leader. (see page 84)

Rapala Knot Use it for attaching the lure to your leader. It forms a small eye, allowing the lure to move freely. (see page 84)

These few knots will meet all your needs. Learn them thoroughly and tie them with care. Always moisten knots in monofilament before smoothly pulling them tight, or the friction heat will change the molecular structure of the line and weaken it dramatically. Accurately applied spit is good for this. Inspect the knot. Does it look right? If not, cut it off and tie it again until it does. Nothing beats a pair of nail clippers for nipping off the ends of monofilament.

The Uni-knot

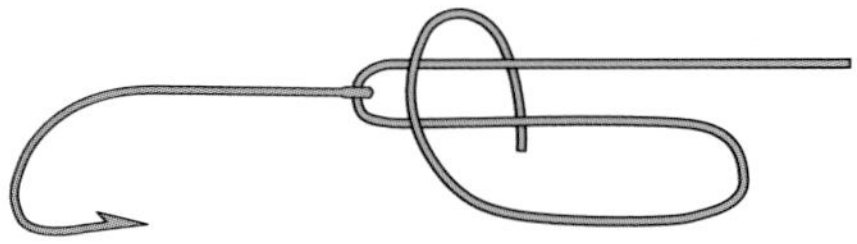

1. Pass the line though the hook's eye and form a loop as shown here.

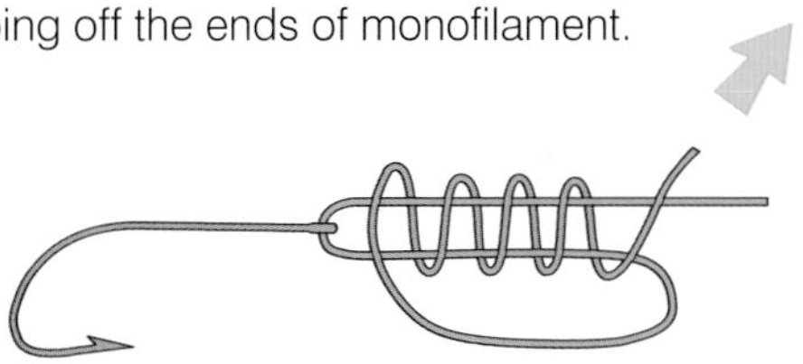

2. Now make at least 4 turns (more for light lines) around both strands and through the loop. Wet the knot with saliva and start tightening it by first pulling on the tag end in the direction of the arrow.

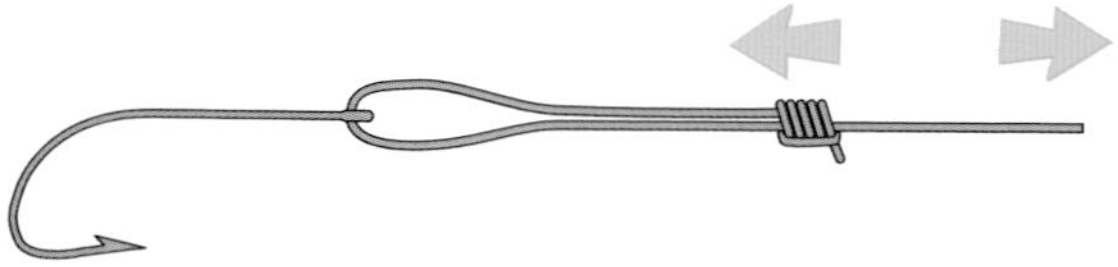

3. With the knot now well consolidated, snip the end off close and pull on the line to slide it down towards the hook.

4. The finished uni-knot.

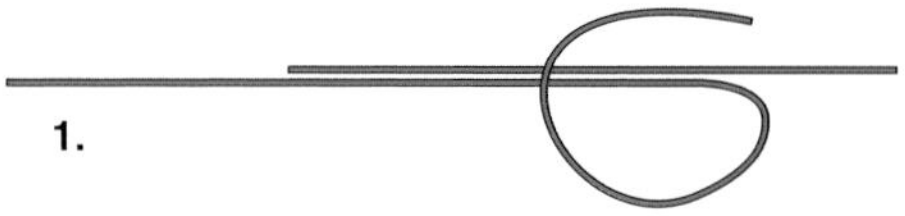

1.

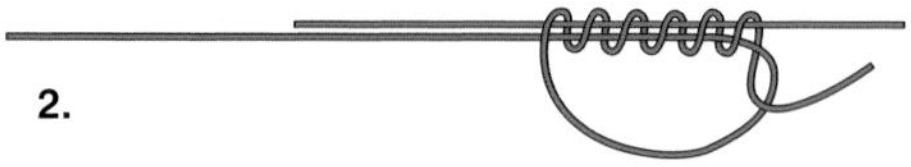

2.

This variant of the uni-knot is a simple way of joining together two lines of approximately the same size. Each line ties a uni-knot around the other before the two are knots pulled together to complete the join.

3.

4.

The Braid knot

1. Double the line and pass the resulting loop through the eye of the hook.

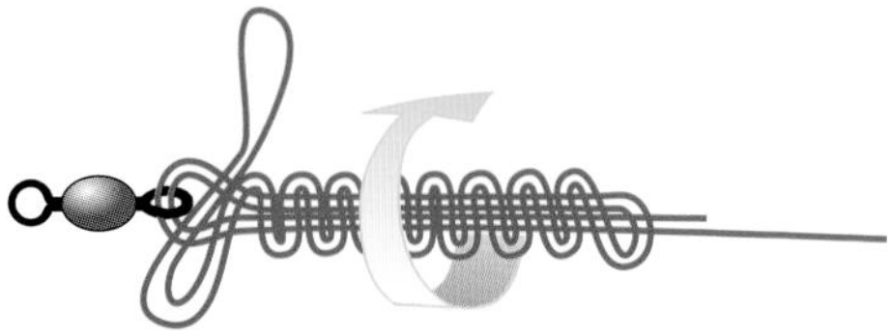

2. From a point a few centimetres from the eye, take about 8-10 turns back toward the hook, finally threading the doubled line through the gap between the turns and the eye.

3. Lubricate in the usual way and pull tight with a steady, continuous motion.

The Snood knot

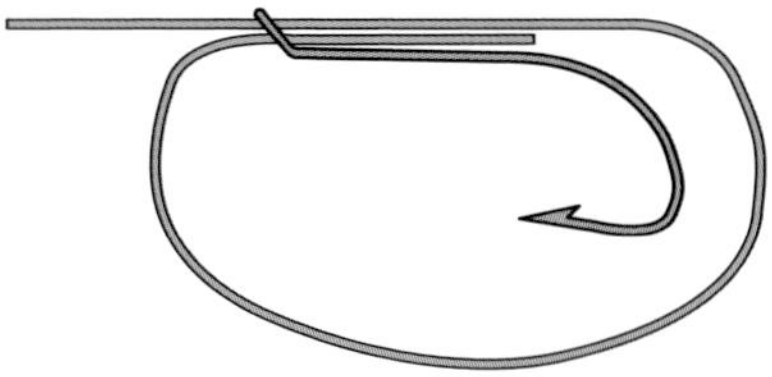

1. Pass the line through the hook's eye twice, as shown here. Note the loop hanging under the hook.

2. Take the loop and wind it around the hook's shank and both lines. 5 or so turns for heavy lines, perhaps 10 for the lightest. To tighten the knot, grip the turns between thumb and forefinger and pull the line in the direction of the arrow.

The Blood loop

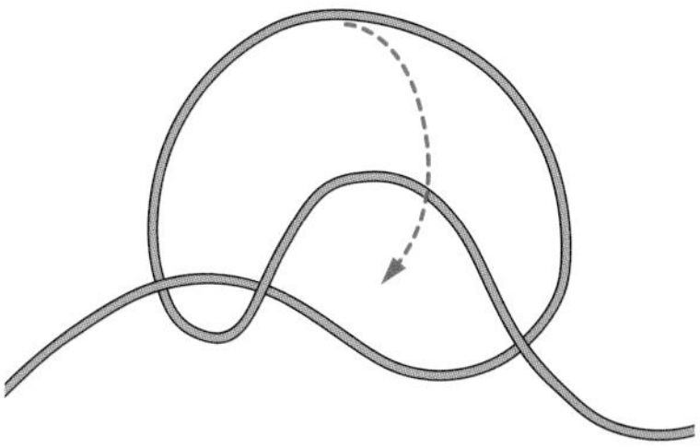

1. There are various types of blood loop but this antipodean variant is one of the strongest. Form a simple loop like this, then take the top of the loop and ...

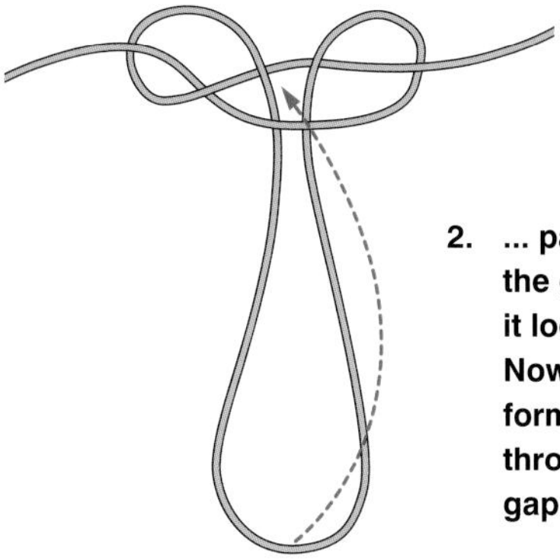

2. ... pass it through the gap shown so it looks like this. Now take the loop formed and pass it through the square gap shown.

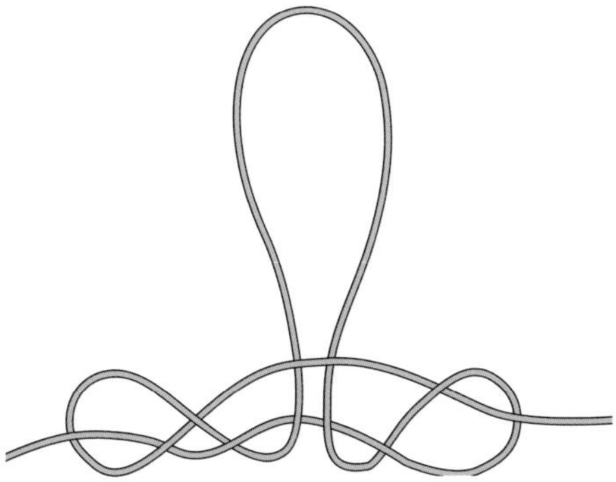

3. You could repeat this process to give added security but for most purposes you've done enough. So ....

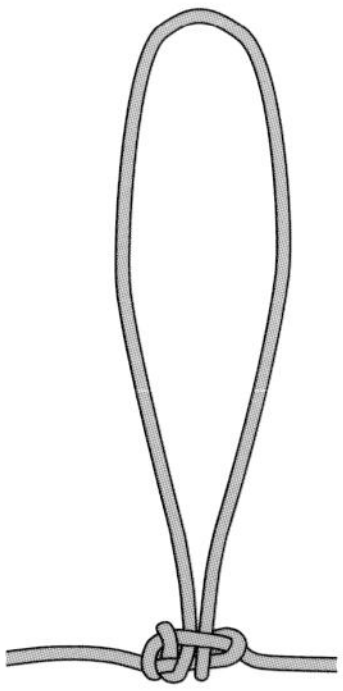

4. .... lubricate with saliva and work the knot tight.

The Albright Special knot

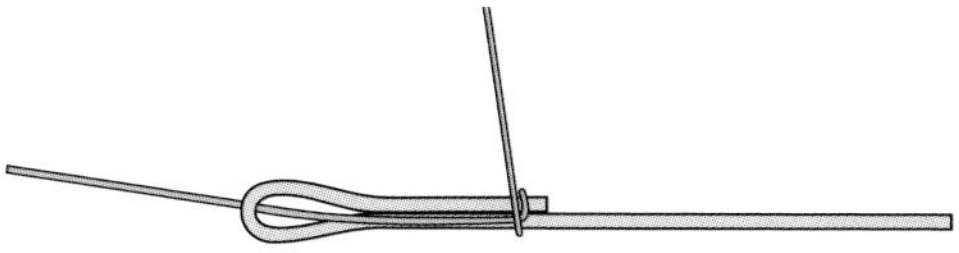

1. Double back the end of the leader and thread the line through the eye produced.

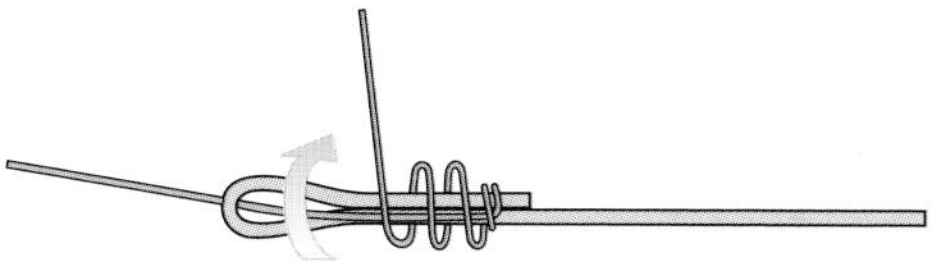

2. Start whipping back over both the line and the leader.

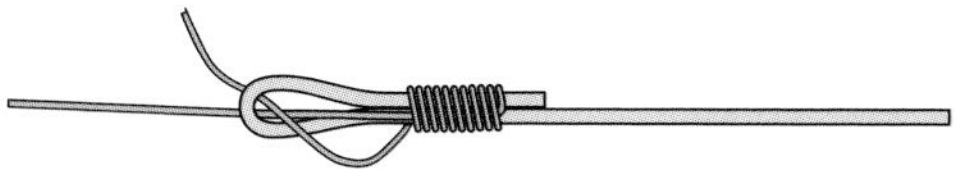

3. Take about 10 turns before poking the line end through the same way it entered. Then....

4. .... lubricate with spit before pulling the knot tight.

The Haywire twist

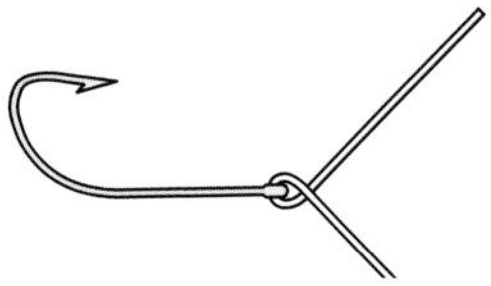

1. Pass about 100mm of wire through the hook's eye and carefully fold back so that it crosses the standing part.

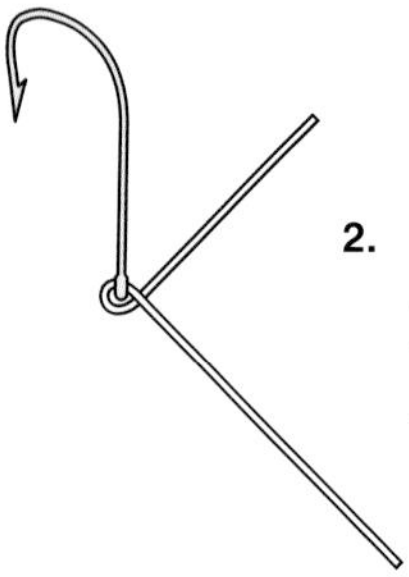

2. Start twisting the wire evenly so each strand turns around the other. The hook can be swivelled to 90° to give some leverage.

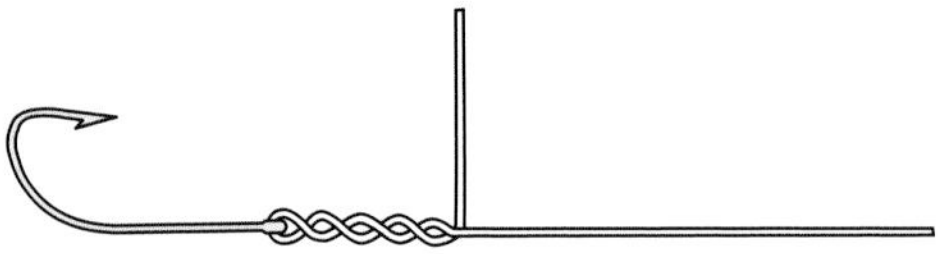

3. After half a dozen twists, bend the tag end upwards so it's perpendicular to the standing part and ....

4. ... add half a dozen turns of 'barrel wraps'. Don't snip off the tag end with pliers or it will leave a sharp spur. Instead, bend the end to form a small crank handle, then twist it back and forth until it breaks.

The Flemish eye

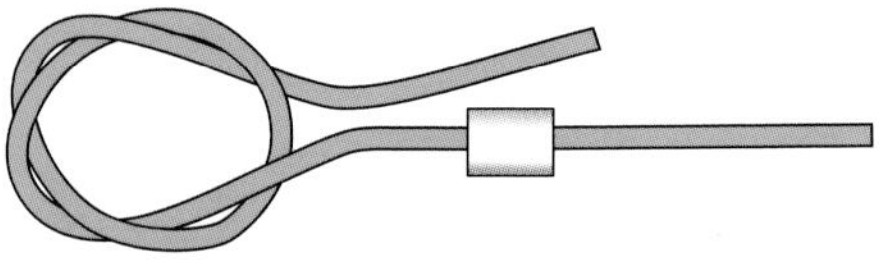

1. Slide a sleeve over the wire. Make an overhand knot then tuck the end through one more time.

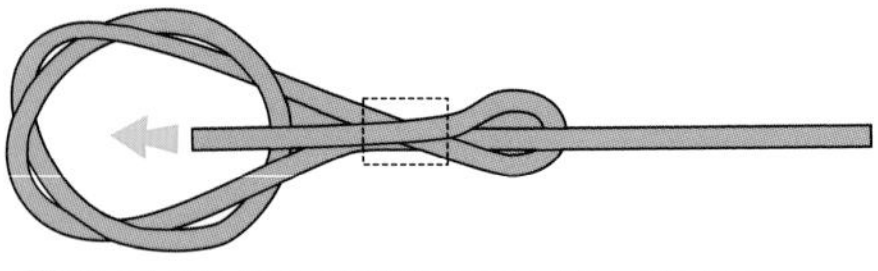

2. Thread the tag end through the sleeve, around the standing part and back through the sleeve. Pull it tight as shown (you might need pliers for this).

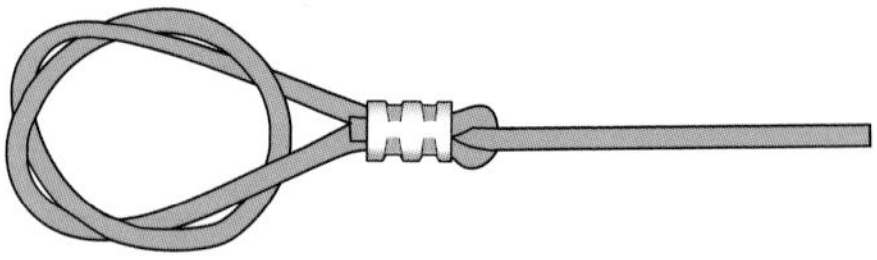

3. Compress the crimp to secure it all before trimming off the tag end. Job done.

As as alternative, you can do without that third pass through the sleeve and simply crimp on a second sleeve instead.

The Rapala knot

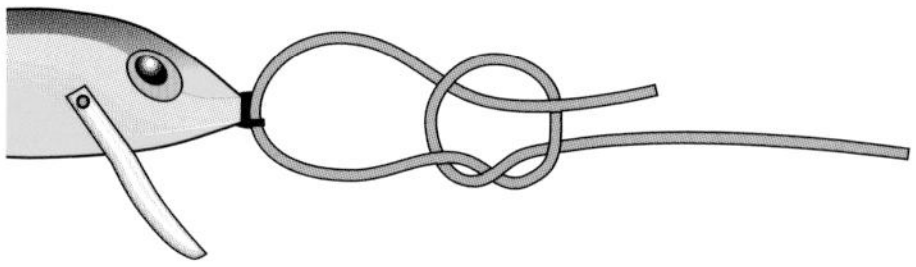

1. First tie an overhand knot and pass the tag end through the lure's eye.

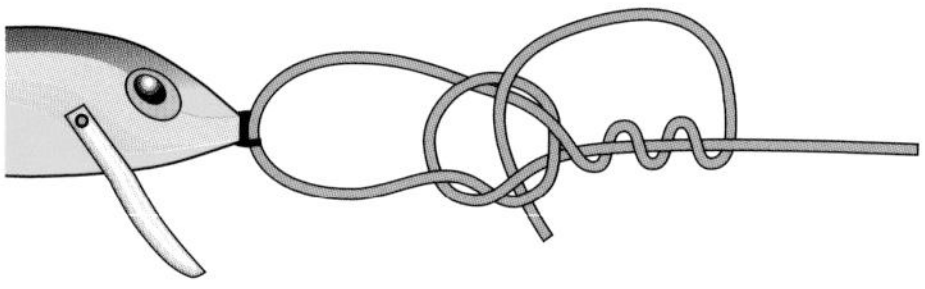

2. Wrap the tag end three times around the standing part of the line before tucking it back through the overhand knot as shown.

3. Next pass the tag end back through the loop you've formed ....

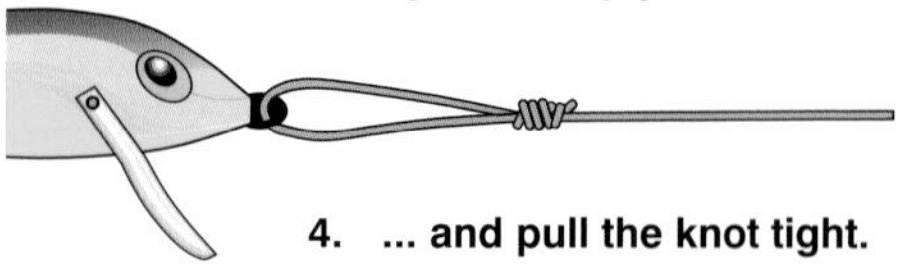

4. ... and pull the knot tight.

CRIMPED CONNECTIONS

Crimps, also known as sleeves or swages, are used for making connections in large diameter mono leaders and all sizes of cable, whether or not nylon coated. I'll call them sleeves from here on in, to avoid any verb/noun confusion. It's important that the correct diameter of sleeve is used – the leader should fit snugly inside but be capable of being easily drawn through the sleeve prior to crimping up the connection. You can't use too small a sleeve – the leader simply won't fit, but you can go too large. Then you will have to over-crimp the sleeve to get it to hold at all, resulting in a very unreliable connection.

There are three styles of sleeves in common use:

- **Round section**
- **Oval section**
- **Figure-of-eight, or double-barrelled section**

As mentioned earlier, using anything other than the correct crimping tool will result in an inferior, unreliable connection. A standard use version is all you'll need and won't cost a great deal. Mine accommodates four different size sleeves up to 2.2mm diameter.

The following table relates sleeve sizes to line strengths:

Sleeve dia	Mono	Cable
0.7mm	40lb to 60lb	50lb to 70lb
0.8mm	50lb to 80lb	60lb to 100lb
0.9mm	60lb to 90lb	70lb to 110lb
1.0mm	80lb to 100lb	100lb to 150lb
1.3mm	100lb to 150lb	200lb to 300lb
1.6mm	150lb to 250lb	300lb to 500lb
1.9mm	250lb to 350lb	500lb to 700lb
2.2mm	400lb to 500lb	700lb to 900lb

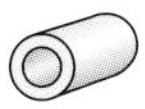

Round Section Sleeves

This is clearly not the best section to snugly contain two parts of the leader, side by side. They can only be compressed using a point-to-cup type of crimping tool. This plier-type tool has various cup shaped indentations on one jaw, and a matching series of rounded points on the other. In use they squeeze the sleeve around the leader, but the contact made isn't uniform – even less so if the leader is crossed inside the sleeve. This type isn't well suited to heavy load applications.

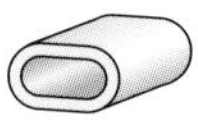

Oval Section Sleeves

This section approximates more closely to that of the doubled-up leader and results in a more secure connection than a round section sleeve. A cup-to-cup crimping tool is used to compress these.

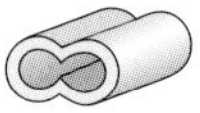

Figure-of-Eight, or Double-barrelled Section Sleeves

This is the way to go in my opinion. Now the two parts of the leader are separate, one in each barrel of the sleeve, eliminating any possible cross-over. The snuggest possible fit is obtained, and the resulting connection is very secure. They are compressed using the cup-to-cup tool, but it's vital that the sleeve is located correctly in the tool. It's tempting to lay the sleeve in two adjacent cups on one jaw and then operate the tool. This is wrong, and won't work. Turn the sleeve through 90° so that it is located within a single cup in each jaw, and compress it through its longest axis.

Sleeves are usually sold in one of two materials – aluminium or copper, but nickel and less frequently brass ones are sometimes seen. Aluminium and stainless steel are at opposite ends of the galvanic table, and aluminium being at the least noble end will corrode galvanically when immersed in seawater. Consequently never use aluminium sleeves on cable leaders. These are intended for use on mono only. However, copper sleeves can be used on mono, but are more likely to cut or damage the line than aluminium ones.

Making a Crimped Connection in Mono

First select a suitable sleeve and thread the line through one barrel. If you intend to reinforce the loop —and it's not a bad idea – slide a short piece of plastic rig tubing over the line before returning it through the other barrel from the opposite direction. If you meant to use the loop to connect to a hook or a swivel, then you should have threaded the line through the eye of the hardware before completing the loop. Otherwise you'll feel very silly having made the perfect crimped loop with nothing in it. Note that I'm assuming the use of a double-barrelled sleeve here. For the moment leave about 50mm or so of the tag end projecting through the sleeve. Melt the very end of the line with a cigarette lighter, and press it lightly against a hard surface to flatten it. Now readjust the loop to the desired size, ensuring that the flattened tag end is drawn up close to the sleeve. Take the crimping tool and select the appropriate cup, but before going any further decide how many times you need to crimp the sleeve.

For example, the 1.3mm diameter sleeves I use are 7mm long, and the 2.2mm diameter ones 13mm long. The jaws of the crimping tool are 4mm wide. So for the smaller ones I crimp them once, leaving flared ends of around 1.5mm at either end. For the larger ones, I crimp them twice, leaving similar flare ends and with a short un-crimped section in the middle of the sleeve. It's important that you don't crimp right to the end of the sleeve, as you risk damaging the line. Check that the sleeve is located correctly in the tool then smoothly squeeze the jaws together.

Making a Crimped Connection in Cable

This is pretty much the same process as making one in mono, other than the tag end melting bit. It's important that you leave no exposed tag end in cable, as it can cause quite nasty cuts. Some anglers intentionally leave a longish tag end, then contain the very end in a second sleeve.

CHAPTER 5

Preparing your catch for the table

Many skippers will tell you that nothing beats a grilled mackerel, fresh from the sea. Maybe they haven't tasted a dorado, but their point is well made; the fresher, the better.

All fish should be gutted and gilled as soon as possible to slow down the process of decay. A large, hard fighting fish will be completely exhausted by the time you have got it in the cockpit. During the fight, lactic acid will have built up in its muscle fibre, and can potentially spoil the flesh. Bleeding the fish will remove it.

Let's imagine the fish that now lies twitching on your cockpit sole is a pelagic gamefish of the open ocean; a wahoo or tuna say. The Jack Iron Rum has done its job, you've removed the lure from the fish's mouth and you're about to bleed the fish before its heart finally stops beating. This will involve sharp knives and demand your closest attention. If there's much of a sea running, you may wish to think about heaving-to.

For protection against knife cuts, special fishing gauntlets are available, constructed with a cut-resistant stainless steel core wrapped in a high-tech polyester and vinyl material (see mackerel photo on page 11).

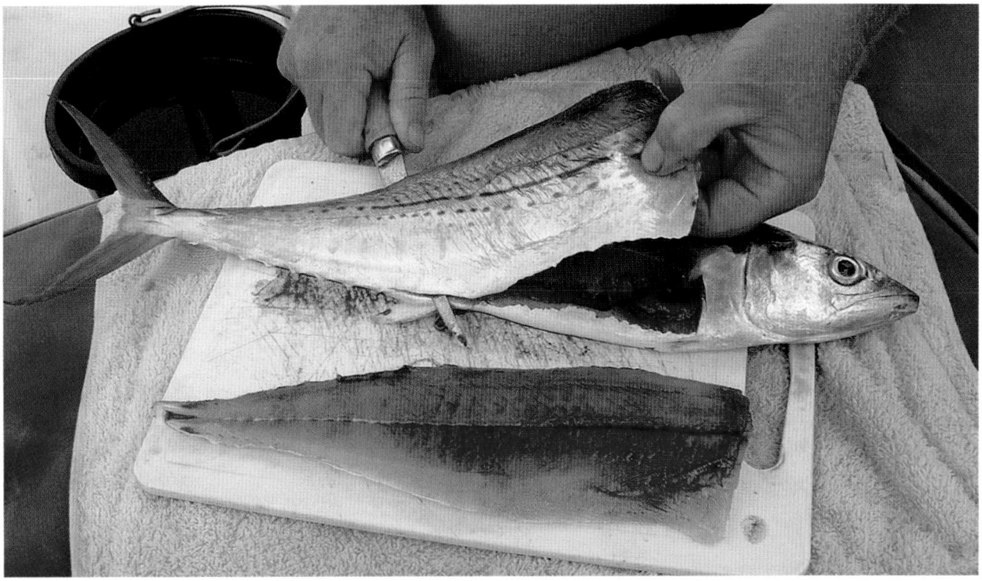

Filleting a Spanish Mackerel

Bleeding

Make a short cut about 75mm (3in) aft of the pectoral fin, deep enough to sever the major blood vessel that runs under the skin in this area. Now slice into the pale area along the lower edge of the gill cover, cutting the blood vessel that supplies the gills. Roll the fish over and make similar cuts on the other side. Now make a final transverse cut on the underside of the fish some 75mm (3in) or 100mm (4in) from the root of the tail. Blood should flow freely from each of these cuts as soon as you make them. If it doesn't, make the cut deeper, longer or in a slightly different position.

The most effective location of these cuts will vary from species to species, but knowledge comes with practice. Now tie a rope around the root of the tail (or through the gills) and trail the fish astern for a few minutes to give it a good flush through. Keep an eye out for sharks! This is an ideal time to swill a few buckets of seawater down the cockpit, which will be looking fairly colourful. You'll probably be reminded at this point that you should have stowed the cockpit cushions below before boating the fish.

Gutting

Haul your fish back over the transom carefully. You'll need to gut it without delay, as the bacteria living there will rapidly cause the flesh to deteriorate if you don't. So how do you want to prepare your fish for the table – in fillets, leave it whole with head on or off, or as cutlets?

For each of these alternatives, the first two steps are:

1. **Remove all fins (but not the tail) with a knife or heavy-duty scissors. This not only gets rid of most of the nasty spiky bits, but also makes step 2 easier.**
2. **Grip the fish by the root of the tail and remove all the scales with the back of a strong knife or a scaler, scraping from stern to bow. If you intend to fillet and skin the fish, there's of course no need to de-scale it. Smaller fish, such as sardines, flying fish, mackerel and bonito are very easily filleted.**

Here's how:

3. **With your very sharp, flexible bladed filleting knife make a first cut just astern of the operculum, slicing down until the blade touches the fish's backbone. Then turn the blade and slice along the backbone to the fish's tail. You now have one fillet.**
4. **Turn the fish over and repeat step 3. You now have two fillets.**
5. **For each fillet, insert the knife blade close to the rib bones and slice the entire section away. You should now be left with two boneless fillets. Any remaining bones can be withdrawn with pliers or tweezers.**
6. **Optional this, but if you want skinless fillets lay the fillet skin-side down on a board and starting from the tail-end, ease the flesh away from the skin with the knife.**

For larger fish you'll need to modify step three as follows:

3. **As before, make a first cut just astern of the gill cover, slicing down until the blade touches the fish's backbone. Now make a separate shallow cut along the length of the fish just off to one side of where the dorsal fin was before you cut it off. Then progressively deepen this cut until you reach the fish's backbone, ending up with the top half of the fillet cut free. Now re-insert the blade in the first cut, turn it and slice along the backbone to the tail, releasing one fillet. Do the same for the other side and you've got two fillets.**

But if you prefer your fish whole, and have got a grill large enough for it:

3. **Slit the underbelly from the vent to a point between the gills, cut the gut as close to the gills as you can and again at the vent, then remove them. Take care not to rupture anything, particularly the green gall bladder which would otherwise contaminate the flesh with foul-tasting gall.**
4. **You will see a dark red vein-like strip running alongside the underside of the backbone. This is the fish's kidney; it must be removed. Use your thumbnail, or if necessary ease it away with the point of a knife.**
5. **If you want to leave the head on, the gills must be removed, as these are almost as rich a source of flesh-rotting bacteria as the guts. Open the operculum, cut through the bone under the lower jaw, snip the gills off top and bottom with a heavy-duty pair of scissors and remove. Otherwise, cut off the head just astern of the gills, remembering to salvage the triangular nuggets of succulent flesh just aft of the eyes.**
6. **Wash out thoroughly in clean seawater and dry with a cloth, then store it in the fridge until you're ready to cook it. If you prefer, rinse it in freshwater immediately prior to cooking.**

Large, round section fish such as tuna and wahoo are best cut into steaks (or cutlets) about 25mm (1in) thick. To cut through the backbone you'll need a meat cleaver or machete coupled with a smart blow from a mallet or similar implement. If fish soup is on the menu, save the head and any other suitable morsels from the carcass.

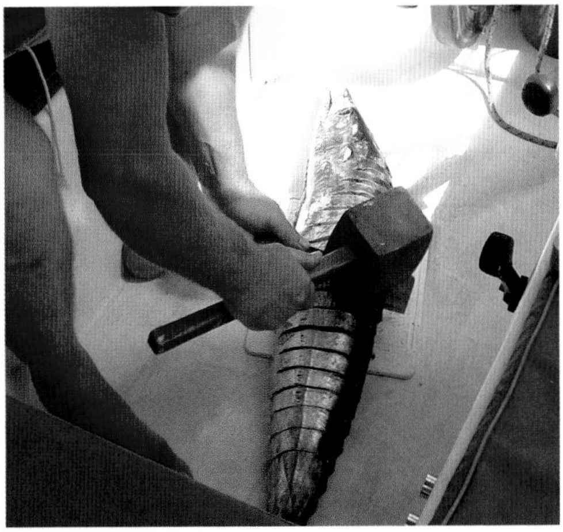

Flatfish

Flatfish, such as plaice, flounder and sole need to be dealt with slightly differently. These fish start out life in a normal vertical plane but at an early stage opt for a horizontal life style on the seabed. This makes one of their eyes largely redundant, so it migrates around to the upper side where it can be of use. Flatfish are best cooked whole or filleted.

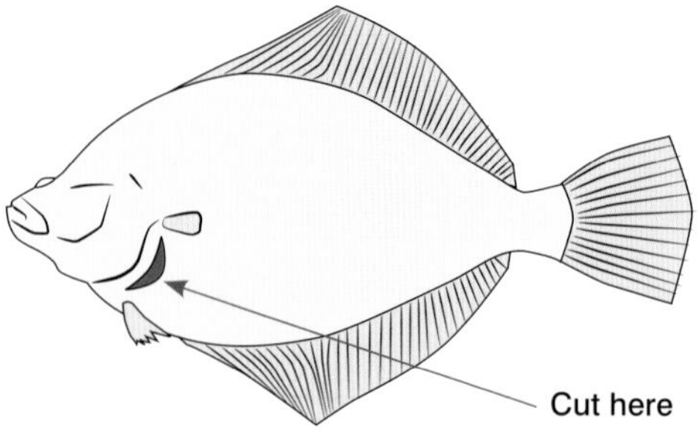
Cut here

Gutting flatfish calls for a special technique. Turn the fish over so that its paler underbody is uppermost. Feel for a soft area immediately behind its head and make a short (depends on the size of the fish) cut there. Reach in and back towards the tail with a finger and hook the guts out.

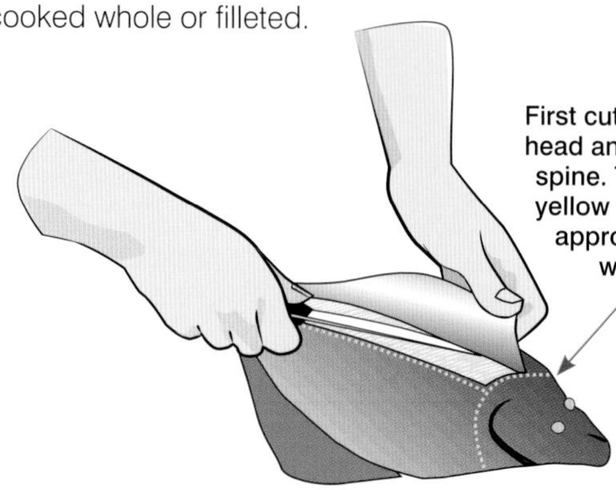
First cut behind the head and along the spine. The dotted yellow lines show approximately where.

Larger flatfish can be filleted. Lay the fish down, right side up and with the tail pointing towards you. Make vertical cuts along the yellow Y-shaped line and then start separating each fillet using a very sharp knife with the blade held almost flat. You should get four fillets from every fish.

Skates and Rays

These similar species are dealt with in the same way. Don't bother with scaling or gutting them. The wings are the edible parts; just cut them off and dispose of the rest. Skinning them is difficult, and is best done after cooking. Stingrays have an antisocial habit of arching their tail over their bodies and inflicting nasty injuries to anyone within striking distance so, as with shark and moray eels, I cut the line as close to the fish as I can and bid it my fond farewell.

Cephalopods, that's squid, cuttlefish and octopi, are of course entirely different. We'll take them in turn.

Squid

Lay the squid on a chopping board, grasp the mantle with one hand and the tentacles with the other, and pull gently apart. Inside the mantle you'll find the quill, which closely resembles a man-made plastic. But it isn't – it's pure squid, so you can throw it over the side. Cut the head off, just downstream of the eyes. Keep the tentacles and the mantle and commit the rest to the deep. Remove the beak from between the tentacles, skin the mantle with your fingers and pull off the wings. Give it all a rinse, dry it on kitchen paper or a clean cloth, and put it in the fridge until you're ready for cooking.

Cuttlefish

Just like a squid, but to the delight of budgies everywhere, you'll find a cuttlebone instead of a quill.

Octopus

The classic Greek way to kill an octopus is to bite it just behind the eyes. This severs the main nerve and kills it instantly, but the risk of being bitten back is very real for all but the most skilled. It requires a deal of practice to get it right, during which period the trainee will enjoy the intimate sensation of the octopus's tentacular embrace and the release of its black ink into his facial orifices, so be warned. For those of a less sporting nature, stabbing it between the eyes with a pointed knife will pierce the brain and achieve a similar but less spectacular result. Don't spend too much time looking for a quill or cuttlebone, as there isn't one.

Having dispatched your octopus you now need to clean it. Turn the mantle inside out and pull out all the bits you don't like the look of. If your intended pulpo menu includes the words 'con su tinto' retain the ink sac, but otherwise discard everything you find inside. Now remove the eyes with a sharp knife, and casting modesty aside, spread the tentacles to reveal the beak and remove that too.

Unless you enjoy a challenge, the meat must be tenderised before cooking. The traditional Greek approach, who clearly have it in for octopi generally, is to hurl it 100 times against a rock. You could give the beast a thorough thrashing with a wooden mallet, or just simmer it gently in water for 30 or 40 minutes. Alternatively, deep freezing the octopus and allowing it to thaw out slowly also achieves the desired result.

Cooking

Nobody gets to eat better fish than do we cruising sailors. Even the freshest fish on a shoreside fishmonger's slab is hours old at best. It'll very probably have been caught in a net in which it drowned, or been left to suffocate in a fishing boat's hold. It'll have died in a heavily stressed condition, and may well be bruised through rough handling and having been buried under tons of its brethren. It'll certainly not have been bled, unless it's been caught specifically for expensive Japanese-style sushi bars.

So we've got the best there is – it would be a shame to spoil it now. If there's one general rule it's not to overcook it. In fact why cook it at all? Try a slice of raw tuna. It's delicious. Consider how much you would have to pay for it in a London, Paris or New York sushi bar and it'll taste even better. For fish that you're about to cook, here are two further tips:

- **If it's been refrigerated, let it warm up to ambient temperature before it hits the pan, or it won't cook through evenly.**
- **Remove it from any water its been lying in, pat it dry with a cloth or kitchen paper, season it with salt and leave for half an hour or so before cooking. This will improve both texture and flavour.**

On 'Alacazam' we tend to keep things simple, and this includes cooking our fish. Frequently this involves nothing more than lightly coating the griddle or frying pan with olive oil, heating it over the gas to a high temperature, adding the fish, some salt and pepper, maybe a squeeze of lemon juice, turn it over once and that's it. Seared to perfection in less than a few minutes.

SAFETY CONSIDERATIONS

Commercial fishing is considered to be one of the most dangerous of all occupations, and fishing while cruising under sail isn't without its risks. Avoiding risks associated with the process of fishing, such as getting a hook in your flesh, line cuts to your hands, knife cuts, fish handling and sailing inattention are dealt with earlier in the text, but others remain.

Equipping the tender

Tenders feature strongly in sailing accident statistics, and appropriate safety precautions must be taken when fishing from them. As well as wearing lifejackets or buoyancy aids and clipping on the engine kill-cord, standard equipment when fishing should include:

- **an anchor and plenty of rode**
- **a hand-held VHF radio**
- **a bailer**
- **flares**
- **oars**
- **drinking water**

One final point; if your tender is an inflatable, leave the gaff on the yacht and use a landing net. Other risks are associated with eating your catch which, after all is the reason for the whole endeavour.

Stromboid Poisoning

The propensity for fish to 'go off' is well known, and the prospect of food poisoning far out at sea beyond the reach of professional medical attention isn't an attractive one. Many of the pelagic fish we catch at sea are members of the scrombridae family (tunas and mackerel) and these along with dorado and jacks are particularly prone to a form of poisoning known as stromboid (or histamine) poisoning. This occurs through spoilage after death through late or inadequate refrigeration. The resultant toxins in the muscle fibre of the fish aren't destroyed by freezing or cooking.

Initial symptoms suggest an allergic response with facial flushing and sweating, burning-peppery taste sensations about the mouth and throat, dizziness, nausea and headache, and can advance to facial rash, hives, diarrhoea and abdominal cramps. Severe cases may blur vision, and cause respiratory stress and swelling of the tongue. Symptoms usually last for approximately 4 to 6 hours and rarely exceed one to two days.

You can reduce symptoms by giving antihistamines such as Benadryl, Dramamine, or Phenergan which are widely available in pharmacies. These have a long shelf life, and should be kept aboard for emergencies. There may be some benefit from emptying the stomach by inducing vomiting, but this should occur within an hour or so of ingestion to be effective.

Prevention always being preferable to cure, you should eat, freeze or refrigerate your catch within 3 hours to avoid any risk of stromboid poisoning. If you keep the temperature setting of your refrigerator just above zero the very maximum you should keep these fish before cooking is 48hrs. Don't eat any fish that tastes sharp and pungent, and in the case of cartilaginous fish like skates, rays and shark that smell even slightly of ammonia.

Ciguatera Poisoning

Fish that live in the vicinity of tropical reefs may contain the ciquatera toxin. The origin of the toxin is in a marine microalgae called gambierdiscus toxicus, which colonise these reefs. As the toxin moves up the food chain, so it becomes more concentrated in its host. Thus the older and larger the fish, the more of the toxin it will contain. The most likely species to contain the toxin are barracuda, grouper, snapper, jack, and moray eels. Amberjack, kingfish, dorado, parrotfish, surgeonfish, triggerfish, filefish, and porgy are also susceptible, but generally to a lesser degree. As the risk associated with ciguatera is both geographical and time related, local knowledge must be gained before eating any of these species. In the West Indies we eat small barracuda caught south of Guadeloupe, but wouldn't look at one of any size in the Virgin Islands.

If you've eaten a fish containing the toxin you'll usually know within 24 hours, often much sooner, early symptoms being vomiting and diarrhoea. This may be followed by neurological symptoms such as tingling fingers or toes. You may also find that cold things feel hot and hot things feel cold. Ciguatera has no cure, but it's a self-limiting disease. Symptoms usually go away in days or weeks but can last for years.

Poisonous fish

Many species of fish are dangerous to eat, but the most poisonous of all is the puffer fish, also known as the blowfish, globefish or swellfish. The fish's ovaries, eggs, blood, liver intestines, and even its skin, contain a fatally poisonous toxin called tetrodoxin. Less than 0.1g (0.004 oz) is enough to kill an adult in as little as 20 minutes.

But although this fish can cause death, puffers are sometimes used as food. In Japan, where the fishes are called fugu, they must be carefully cleaned and prepared by a specially trained chef. Even so, I would tend to skip the fish course if the offer came my way.

Next on the 'do not eat list' are boxfish and porcupine fish. These, like the puffer fish have the capability to inflate when threatened and have nothing about them that would suggest they are remotely edible. Off the coasts of the UK the ocean sunfish, or mola, are occasionally seen basking on the surface. If you've ever spotted a floppy, shark like dorsal fin on the surface it's probably one of these beauties. The flesh of these migrants from warmer seas is also poisonous, so leave well alone.

Well now I've included a few fishy horror stories to add to all those others we've heard in connection with this wonderful pastime of ours. But we still sail, confident that our skill, knowledge and natural caution will go a long way towards keeping us from harm's way. And so it must be with fish and fishing. Learn at every opportunity, heed the advice of local people and don't eat any species that you don't recognise before finding out if it's safe to do so. As I was once instructed, remember that the most important item of safety equipment on any sailing boat is the one between the skipper's ears.

With this in mind and the few tips and techniques you may have picked up from this book, you'll safely dine on the culinary delights that are there to be had from the ocean.

The following table sets out the line capacities of reels regularly used for trolling:

Alvey Model No.	Spool Diameter	Line Capacity (mono)
456B	115mm (4½")	700m of 9 kg (765yds of 20lb)
520A52	125mm (5")	1,000m of 9 kg (1,090yds yards of 20lb)
550C5	140mm (5½")	900m of 7 kg (975yds of 15lb)
525C52	125mm (5")	1000m of 9 kg (1,090yds of 20lb)
655C52	165mm (6½")	700m of 18 kg (765yds of 40lb)
725C52	180mm (7")	630m of 23 kg (690yds of 50lb)
825BCVC	208mm (8¼")	490m of 23 kg (500 yards of 50lb)
925C52	230mm (9")	800m of 23 kg (875 yards of 50lb)
925CMW	230mm (9")	800m of 23 kg (875 yards of 50lb)

Penn Senator Models	Size	Gear Ratio	Line Capacity (mono)
117L	14/0	1.6:1	685m of 60kg (750yds of 130lb)
116L	12/0	2.0:1	730m of 36 kg (800yds of 80lb)
115L	9/0	2.5:1	615m of 23kg (675yds of 50lb)
114	6/0	2.1:1	480m of 23kg (525yds of 50lb)
113	4/0	2.1:1	435m of 13 kg (475yds of 30lb)
49L Mariner	3/0	3.5:1	435m of 13 kg (475yds of 30lb)

Daiwa Sealine H models	Gear Ratio	Line Capacity (mono)
27SH	4.6:1	200m of 9kg (220yds of 20lb)
300H	3.7:1	210m of 18kg (230yds of 40lb)
350H	3.7:1	260m of 18kg (280yds of 40lb)

Shimano TLD Series model	Gear Ratio	Line Capacity (mono)
TLD-15	5.2:1	330m of 9kg (360yds of 20lb)
TLD-20	3.6:1	415m of 133kg (450yds of 30lb)
TLD-25	3.6:1	415m of 18kg (450yds of 40lb)
TLD-20II	4.0 / 1.7:1	415m of 13kg (450yds of 30lb)
TLD-30II	4.0 / 1.7:1	415m of 18kg (450yds of 40lb)
TLD-50II	3.5 / 1.4:1	650m of 23kg (700yds of 50lb)

YOUR TACKLE BOX

If, as I hope, the previous pages have encouraged you to try your hand at catching fish you'll need to buy a few items of tackle. Whereas just a simple handline might serve to catch mackerel or bass around our shores, for more ambitious angling you will need rather more ambitious tackle.

Ideally, take someone experienced with you on your first foray to the tackle shop, for you should be warned: many of the items on display are designed to catch anglers rather than fish. Remember, you don't have to buy it all at once.

For a tackle box suitable for most fishing afloat situations, here's what I'd recommend:

Tools and equipment

- Beads – various colours and sizes
- Butt pad
- Crimping tool – to suit all sleeve sizes
- Elasticated thread – for use with shellfish baits
- Floats – sliding type
- Hooks – Singles, doubles and trebles. From size 4 fine-wire hooks through to 10/0 for use with baits and artificial lures.
- Hook sharpener – file type or stone
- Ice pick – for killing fish
- Knife
- Knife sharpener
- Leader materials – Mono, plastic-coated multi-strand wire and single-strand wire
- Line clippers – retired nail clippers are ideal
- Loop protectors
- Multi-pliers
- Planers – plastic type (often called paravanes) or stainless steel
- Reel spanners and lubricant – often supplied with reels when first purchased
- Rigging needles
- Rigging wire – copper or monel
- Rubber bands – for use with planer kit
- Scissors
- Sleeves – single and double-barrelled, sizes 0.7mm to 1.9mm
- Spare skirts – for skirted trolling lures, 100mm long and 200mm long in assorted colours
- Swivels – Barrel swivels and those equipped with links (or snaps)
- Unhooking tool

Rods and reels

- General purpose rod, 2.0m to 2.5m long, for casting, jigging and float fishing.
- Fixed spool reel to suit above rod, ideally with two spools, one loaded with 6lb line and the other with 15lb line.
- 50lb trolling rod, around 1.65m long, preferably with a roller top ring as a minimum requirement.
- Size 6/0 multiplier reel loaded with 500yds of 50lb line. This is something as a compromise as it's heavy for mackerel and bass, but is the absolute minimum for larger and more powerful offshore fish.

Artificial lures

No tackle box should be without a selection of these, which can be used with your general purpose outfit, either for jigging or light trolling.

- **Hokkais**
- **Muppets**
- **Jellyworms**
- **Shads**
- **Redgills**
- **Jigs**

And also for use with your general purpose outfit, a selection of plugs designed for casting and operating a specific depths:

Yo-Zuri Hydro Tiger	Surface lure
Yo-Zuri Mag Popper	Surface lure
Yo Zuri 3D Popper	Surface lure
Yo-Zuri Banana Boat	Surface lure
X-Rap Super Shad	Suspending lure
Yo-Zuri Mag Darter	Floating/Diving, up to 1m deep
Yo-Zuri Crystal Minnow	Floating/Diving, up to 1.5m deep
Yo-Zuri 3D Crank	Floating/Diving, up to 3.5m deep
Yo-Zuri Crystal Minnow Deep Diver	Floating/Diving, up to 6m deep
Rapala Rattlin' Rapala	Sinking, 1.5m to 2.5m
Yo-Zuri Hardcore Shad	Sinking, 1.5m to 2.5m
Yo-Zuri Emperor Minnow	Sinking, 1.5m to 2m

For offshore trolling you'll need a selection of skirted lures, spoons, plugs and, if your budget's up to it, soft plastic lures.

Skirted Lures

Williamson Dorado Catcher	Flat-faced pusher
Williamson Wahoo Catcher	Jethead
Williamson Dorado Jig	Combined Octopus/Squid skirt and tuna feather

Spoons

Drone spoon	Best fished slow and deep
Pet spoon	Best fished slow and deep

Plugs

Yo-Zuri Surface Cruiser	Skitters along on surface, trolling speed 2knots to 4knots
Yo-Zuri Bonita	Running depth 1.5m to 2.5m, trolling speed 2knots to 8knots
Rapala Sliver	Running depth 2.7m to 3.3m, trolling speed 2knots to 8knots.
Rapala Barra Magnum	Running depth 3.5m to 5.4m, trolling speed 2knots to 8knots
Rapala Count Down Magnum	Running depth 2.7m to 7.5m, trolling speed 6knots to 12knots
Rapala X-Rap Magnum 15	Running depth 3m to 4.5m, trolling speed 6knots to 12knots
Rapala X-Rap Magnum 30	Running depth 6m to 9m, trolling speed 6knots to 12knots
Rapala X-Rap Magnum 20	Running depth 4.5m to 6m, trolling speed 6knots to 12knots
Yo-Zuri Hydro Magnum	Running depth 4.5m to 6m, trolling speed 6knots to 12knots

Soft plastic lures

Williamson Live Series Mackerel (7")	Best trolled between 2knots and 6knots
Williamson Live Series Ballyhoo (8½")	Best trolled between 2knots and 8knots

Bird	A teaser designed to splash around on the surface ahead of your trolled lure.
Ciquatera toxin	A toxin sometimes found in reef-associated predatory fish. If eaten, affected fish are poisonous to humans.
Continental shelf	The area of relatively shallow water surrounding the UK and Europe.
Crimper	A tool for compressing crimps around the line.
Crimps	Also known as sleeves or swages, these are used to form connections in heavy mono or multi-strand cable where a knot is impractical.
Daisy chain	A string of plastic skirted lures, only the end one of which contains a hook, the others acting as teasers.
Demersal	Fish species that feed on creatures that live on the sea bed.
Down-rigger	A cranelike device which lowers a planer to a pre-determined depth.
Dropper	A short hook link attached above a weight or lure.
FAD	Fish Aggegation Device - a floating platform under which fish congregate, used by commercial fishermen.
Fixed-spool reel	A reel type primarily intended for casting where the spool doesn't rotate and a bale arm winds the line around the spool.
Gaff	A tool comprising a handle and a sharp hook for boating your catch.
Jig	An artificial lure designed to be fished vertically in the water column, a method known as jigging.
Joey	An immature mackerel - likely to be unruly and rude to its parents.
Leader	A length of line to which a hook or lure is attached, of different breaking strain and/or material than the main line.
Leadhead	A lure comprising a metal head and fixed hook, to which soft-plastic bodies are attached.
Ledger	A rig involving a sliding weight designed to present a bait on the seabed.
Mantle	The body part of a squid from which the head and tentacles emerge.
Monel	A corrosion-resistant metal. Wire made from it.
Mono	Nylon monofilament line.
Multiplier	A reel type which relies on internal gearing to increase the spool/ handle rotation above 1:1.

Muppet	A soft-plastic imitation squid.
Operculum	The gill-cover of a fish.
Paravane	A plastic or steel device designed to dive when dragged through the water. Used instead of a weight when trolling to fish the lure at increased depth.
Paternoster	A rig designed to be fished on or close to the seabed, comprising a lead weight and one or more droppers attached above it.
Pectoral fin	The fin immediately aft of the gill cover.
Pelagic	The fish of the open ocean, not resident to any specific area or feature.
Pirk	A heavy chrome-plated jig-type lure designed to descend quickly and often used when fishing over deepwater wrecks.
Planer	See Paravane
Plug	A trolling or casting lure, designed to imitate – in appearance and action - a small baitfish.
Shad	A small soft-plastic fish-shaped lure.
Sinker	A weight attached to the line.
Sleeves	See Crimps.
Snood	A short hook link. See also Dropper.
Snubber	A shock-absorber incorporated in a handline.
Spinner	A small rotating metal lure.
Split shot	Small weights squeezed onto the line, used with light float tackle.
Spreader bar	An array of plastic skirted lures attached to a metal bar, designed as a decoy imitating a small shoal of fish.
Stinger	A secondary hook, intended to catch short-striking fish.
Stromboid toxin	A form of poisoning caused by eating fish that has started to 'go off'.
Swages	See Crimps.
Swivel	A small metal device connected between lure and the end of the main line which allows any twists to unwind.
Teaser	Any device designed to attract fish to your lure, and induce them to strike.
Trolling	Towing a lure astern when underway.

1 **Important** To help us comply with Data Protection legislation, please tick ***either*** Box A or Box B (you must tick Box A to ensure you receive the full benefits of RYA membership). The RYA will not pass your data to third parties.

☐ **A.** I wish to join the RYA and receive future information on member services, benefits and offers by post and email.

☐ **B.** I wish to join the RYA but do not wish to receive future information on member services, benefits and offers by post and email.

When completed, please send this form to: RYA, RYA House, Ensign Way, Hamble, Southampton, SO31 4YA

2

	Title	Forename	Surname	Date of Birth	Male	Female
1.				DD / MM / YY		
2.				DD / MM / YY		
3.				DD / MM / YY		
4.				DD / MM / YY		

Address

Town **County** **Post Code**

Evening Telephone **Daytime Telephone**

email

Signature:............................ **Date:**............................

3 Type of membership required: *(Tick Box)*

☐ ***Personal*** *Annual rate £39 or £36 by Direct Debit*

☐ ***Under 21*** *Annual rate £13 (no reduction for Direct Debit)*

☐ ***Family**** *Annual rate £58 or £55 by Direct Debit*

** Family Membership: 2 adults plus any under 21s all living at the same address*

4 Please tick ONE box to show your main boating interest.

☐ Yacht Racing
☐ Dinghy Racing
☐ Personal Watercraft
☐ Powerboat Racing
☐ Motor Boating
☐ Yacht Cruising
☐ Dinghy Cruising
☐ Inland Waterways
☐ Windsurfing
☐ Sportsboats and RIBs

Please see Direct Debit form overleaf

RYA

Instructions to your Bank or Building Society to pay by Direct Debit

Please complete this form and return it to:
Royal Yachting Association, RYA House, Ensign Way, Hamble, Southampton, Hampshire SO31 4YA

DIRECT Debit

1. To The Manager: Bank/Building Society

Address:

Post Code:

2. **Name(s) of account holder(s)**

3. **Branch Sort Code**

__ __ — __ __ — __ __

4. **Bank or Building Society account number**

Originators Identification Number

9	5	5	2	1	3

5. **RYA Membership Number (For office use only)**

6. **Instruction to pay your Bank or Building Society**
Please pay Royal Yachting Association Direct Debits from the account detailed in this instruction subject to the safeguards assured by The Direct Debit Guarantee.
I understand that this instruction may remain with the Royal Yachting Association and, if so, details will be passed electronically to my Bank/Building Society.

Signature(s) ________________

Date ________________

Banks and Building Societies may not accept Direct Debit instructions for some types of account

Cash, Cheque, Postal Order enclosed
Made payable to the Royal Yachting Association

£

077

Office use only: Membership Number Allocated

Office use / Centre Stamp

Join The Green Blue...

...in protecting our coasts and waterways.

Each time we use, clean or maintain our boat we may be harming the beautiful environment we are out to enjoy. The good news is that it there are simple things everyone can do to prevent this. Follow our 'top tips' to ensure that your conscience is as clean as your boat!

EFFECTS ON WILDLIFE

Find out whether the areas you visit are protected and why. There may be vulnerable seabed species, so beware of dragging your anchor.

OIL AND FUEL SPILLS

Good maintenance of fuel lines, connections and seals helps avoid leaks. Check bilge water for contaminants before routine pumping.

ANTIFOULING & MARINE PAINTS

Only scrub off the fouling, not the paint and encourage your marina, club or boatyard to collect & properly dispose of wash down residues.

WASTE MANAGEMENT

Don't throw anything over the side, including food; even orange peel can take up to 2 years to decompose in the water.

RESOURCE EFFICIENCY

The latest generation of wind generators are quiet, efficient and a great way to charge your batteries.

CLEANING AND MAINTENANCE

Replacing acidic teak cleaners with a mild soap and abrasive pad is not only better for the environment but eliminates solvents which may damage seam compounds.

British Marine Federation

RYA

THE CROWN ESTATE

More tips and advice can be found on our website: www.thegreenblue.org.uk

Read the Environmental Code of Practice to find out how your club can reduce its impact on the environment: www.ecop.org.uk

THE GREEN BLUE
RYA House, Ensign Way,
Hamble, Southampton
SO31 4YA
Tel: 023 8060 4227
www.thegreenblue.org.uk
info@thegreenblue.org.uk

NOTES

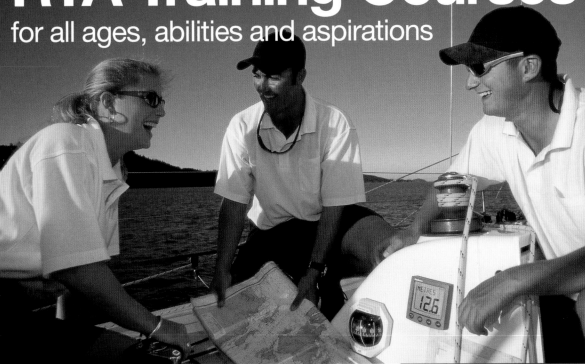

getheknowledge

RYA books for preparation

RYA Weather Handbook Northern Hemisphere

Chris Tibbs

Explains how to interpret area weather forecasts, modify them for local conditions and improve on their accuracy. Official RYA reference book to accompany the revised Yachtmaster syllabus.

G1

RYA Knots, Splices & Ropework

Gordon Perry and Steve Judkins

Perfect for everyone wanting to learn about knots or increase their knotting knowledge. Structured around three main steps, providing essential information from learning the ropes to advanced knotting.

G63

RYA Navigation Handbook

Tim Bartlett

An essential course book for RYA Training courses, this title delves into the art of navigation, both electronic and traditional, giving equal weight to the needs of both power and sailing vessels.

G6

RYA Diesel Engine Handbook

Andrew Simpson

Develops knowledge and confidence required by diesel engine boat owners and those taking the RYA one day Diesel Engine Course. Includes CD-Rom.

G25

RYA An Introduction to Radar

This handy little book follows the syllabus of the RYA One-Day Radar Course and is ideal for anyone requiring a working knowledge of radar.

G34

RYA VHF Handbook

Tim Bartlett

Explains how to use short range radios to contact coast guards and other boats. It constitutes essential background reading for a VHF course.

G31

RYA Passage Planning

Peter Chennell

Passage planning should always be an integral part to yacht or motor cruising, this informative new title will help you along the way.

G69

To find out more about RYA Publications or to place an order, please visit **www.rya.org.uk/shop** or call **0845 345 0372**

getheknowledge